BOOKS

Arboriculture
&THE LAW

Victor D. Merullo
Michael J. Valentine

There is no substitute for current legal advice. This publication is not intended as, and does not represent, legal advice and should not be relied upon to take the place of such advice. Although every effort has been made to assure the accuracy of the information included in this publication as of the date on which it was issued, laws, court decisions and governmental regulations in the United States are all subject to frequent change.

Composition by Wadley Graphix Corporation
Printed by Kowa Graphics, Inc.

International Society of Arboriculture
P.O. Box GG
Savoy, IL 61874
Phone (217) 328-2032

Foreword

The following article has been republished with the permission of Larry Hall, Editor of *Arbor Topics*, published by Hendricksen, The Care of Trees. This article appeared in the Spring and Summer, 1992, edition of this publication.

"The Rights!? of Trees"

Imagine, if you will, that trees can hire attorneys. Suppose trees are endowed by their creator with certain inalienable rights. Would you relate differently with trees? Consider the following cases.

Bryan Kotwica

Case #1. The Honorable Judge Bristlecone of the Third Circuit Court heard opening arguments today in the case of the Native Oak Grove vs. Scrape and Doze Contracting. The plaintiffs in this case allege the wrongful death and mutilation of members of their family by the defendants. The trees claim that their rights were violated during the construction of human homes in their midst. The trees further claim that it was a willful violation because there was ample evidence that injury would result if the defendants did not take necessary precautions. The trees argue that the defendants committed a crime against Nature and ask the court to impose the best judgement possible. They ask the court to impart respect for Nature into the hearts of the defendants.

Case #2. Criminal conspiracy charges have been filed against a group of defendants in a case involving abuse of young trees. The defendants in this case are several individuals that were involved in the planting of hundreds of young trees. The state alleged that the trees were planted in poor growing environments and were often planted in situations in which they could not adapt. The young trees, it is claimed, were doomed to a poor quality of life and often a slow, painful death. The state's attorney for the environment hopes to gain a judgement requiring people planting trees to fully understand the rights and needs of trees. The state argues that the lives of thousands of trees could be saved if they were planted and maintained properly.

Case #3. Attorneys representing a 150 year old oak tree appeared in court today to answer charges that their client is responsible for injuring a person and damaging property. A large part of the tree fell on a house putting a hole in the roof and slightly injuring a person inside. The tree argues that fault lies with its human neighbors. Because the tree lives in such close proximity to the house, it is the humans' responsibility to provide care for the tree to help insure

iv

the safety of both parties. In return for this care, the tree would provide shade, clean air, and natural beauty. In this particular case the tree indicated a potential hazard well before the damage occurred. A crack was visible in the tree and fruiting bodies of a fungus were growing in plain view. A professional arborist could have prevented the damage to the house and individual and may have been able to save the part of the tree that was lost. Regardless of the outcome of this court procedure, the tree will be removed because of the severe damage it received in this incident. This tree that was alive twenty years before our Civil War wishes only to be exonerated of blame before it is removed by men that were born twenty-five years after the Second World War.

If trees could hire attorneys and assert their rights as living beings, what effect would this have on all of us?

Acknowledgments

The International Society of Arboriculture (ISA) was responsible for assembling a task force of individuals dedicated to the tree care profession who have provided their time and input on the various topics contained in *Arboriculture & The Law*. We want to express our appreciation to Walter S. Barrows, Sr., Eugene Eyerly, Sam Gorlich, Gilbert High, James Mertes, and Peter Tatoian for their dedication and commitment to this project. ISA deserves the credit for their efforts in assembling this task force and coordinating all details necessary in the development and completion of this project.

The Authors

Columbus, Ohio
August, 1992

Table of Contents

INTRODUCTION

It is almost beyond comprehension that something which appears on its face as simple as the everyday common tree could involve so many complex legal issues. The typical landowner generally sees only the beauty that trees bring to the landscape, or the shade that they provide from the blistering rays of the sun. Generally, the typical landowner is not even aware of the legal aspects relating to the trees growing on the landowner's property. This lack of knowledge on the part of the landowner often times prevents the landowner from taking the proper precautions in guarding against some of the responsibilities and liabilities that may result when injuries are caused to person or property by a tree growing on the landowner's property thus causing costly and needless litigation. The landowner's lack of knowledge in relation to trees may also cause the landowner to be unaware of the many rights available when trees have been wrongfully injured or destroyed by another individual or entity.

Private landowners are not the only individuals involved in litigation resulting from incidents relating to trees. Municipalities, public utility companies, private tree companies, practicing arborists and highway agencies are also frequent parties to litigation arising out of incidents relating to trees.

The rights, duties and liabilities that each of the aforesaid parties may have with regard to trees is an area rich with case law. This publication will discuss many of the duties and responsibilities that a landowner, municipality, private tree company, practicing arborist, public utility and public agencies have under various circumstances to prevent injury to person and property caused by trees. This publication will also discuss the rights a property owner has in the event of an unauthorized destruction of trees by either an individual, private tree company, public utility or governmental entity, as well as, the various measures of damages available to the property owner when such an unauthorized destruction occurs.

Chapter 1

Generalized Duty of Care Owed by Landowners in Relation to Trees Growing on Their Property

What duty of care does a land-owner have in the maintenance of trees on the landowner's property?

The current trend in the United States is that the landowner will be held to a duty of care, determined by principles of negligence. The landowner will be held to the duty of common prudence in maintaining trees on the land-owner's property in such a way as to prevent injury to a neighbor's property and person. A brief review of cases dealing with a landowner's duty regarding trees growing on the land-owner's property shows the difficulty which the courts have had in deciding upon issues pertaining to tree-related damages. In the case of *Dudley v. Meadowbrook*,[1] a large tree on the defendants' property fell across an alley and onto the plaintiff's premises, damaging the plaintiff's garage and other property. The Court, in deciding upon the issue of liability, deter-mined that the sound and practical rule is that liability in such cases is to be determined by the test of negligence and that a landowner should be held to the duty of common prudence in maintaining such property, including trees thereon, in such a way as to prevent injury to a neighbor's property.[2]

A similar case outlining the duty of care a landowner will be held to in maintaining trees upon the landowner's property is *Turner v. Ridley*.[3] In *Turner*, an action was brought against a landowner for damage caused when a tree on the landowner's property fell across an abutting public sidewalk striking an automobile parked at the curb. The Court held that a landowner who has actual or constructive knowledge of a patently defective condition of a tree, which may result in injury to a traveler on a highway, must exercise reasonable care to prevent harm from the falling of such tree or its branches on a person lawfully using the highway.[4]

Does it make a difference if a landowner has knowledge of a dangerous condition which exists regarding the landowner's trees?

Yes, as can be seen from both the *Dudley* and *Turner* cases, an issue arises as to whether a landowner will be responsible for damages caused by a tree that falls due to some condition of the tree which the landowner may or may not be aware of. In *Brandywine Hundred Realty Co. v. Cotillo,*[5] the plaintiff was driving an automobile on a road abutting the defendant's land. About ten feet from the road on the defendant's property stood a Chestnut tree. The tree had been dead for four years, but bore no visual exterior evidence of decay. As the plaintiff passed the tree, the tree fell striking the plaintiff's automobile thereby killing the plaintiff's companion.

The Court in *Brandywine* approved the following jury instruction:

> The condition of the tree in question was the result of natural causes; still, if such condition was known or by the exercise of ordinary care could have been known by the defendant, then it became the duty of the defendant to exercise reasonable care and diligence to prevent the tree from falling and injuring those who might have occasion to use the public highway.[6]

It is apparent from the foregoing cases that a landowner is not only held to the duty of common prudence in maintaining trees on the landowner's property, but the landowner is also held to an even greater duty of inspection to discover possible defective conditions of a tree in order to prevent the tree from falling and injuring others.

Is there a difference in liability for a tree of natural growth and one planted by a landowner or the landowner's predecessor?

Yes, a distinction is found to exist relating to liability with regard to trees of natural growth and those planted by the landowner or the landowner's predecessors which overhang on an adjoining landowner's property. For example, in *Griefield v. Gibralter Fire and Marine Ins. Co.*,[7] a lawsuit was brought by the Gibralter Fire and Marine Insurance Company against Angelina M. Griefield. This action was brought to recover an amount which the plaintiff insurance company was compelled to pay to its insured for damages to the insured's house from an overhanging limb of a tree growing on the defendant's land.

In determining whether or not the defendant should be held liable for the damage caused by the overhanging limb, the Court determined that the test for liability was whether the tree limb which overhung the plaintiff's property was of natural growth or had been planted by the defendant or a former possessor of her land. The Court ruled that if the tree had been planted by the defendant or a former possessor of her land, then liability would result. However, if the tree of the defendant was of natural growth, the defendant would not be held liable for the resulting damage.[8]

The Court in *Griefield* relied on the Restatement, Torts Section 840 in making its decision. The relevant provisions of the Restatement, Torts Section 840 relied upon by the Court in *Griefield* were set out in the case of *Sterling v. Weinstein*.[9] In the *Sterling* case, the plaintiff brought an action for damages and for the abatement of a nuisance against the defendant. The action was brought as a result of two rather large trees owned by the defendant which extended over the plaintiff's property causing leaves and bark from the branches to fall onto the plaintiff's building stopping up the gutters.

The Court in construing the Restatement, Torts Section 840 stated: "Where a natural condition of land causes an invasion of another's interest in the use and enjoyment of their land, the possessor of the land containing the natural condition is not liable for such invasion."

Comment (a) under that section states: "natural condition" means a condition "not in any way the result of human activity" and includes "trees, weeds and other vegetation on land which has not been made artificially receptive thereto by act of man."

Illustration 4 under that section reads: "A purchases and takes possession of land on which have been planted a number of eucalyptus trees near the boundary line of B's land. The roots of the eucalyptus trees grow into B's land with the result that walnut trees growing thereon are stunted and otherwise damaged. Although A knows of this he does not cut down the eucalyptus trees. A is subject to the rule stated in Section 840, since the eucalyptus trees are not a natural condition."[10]

Therefore, it would appear that the Restatement would make liability with regard to a tree which overhangs upon the property of another rest on whether or not the offending tree in a particular case is a natural condition of the land. As was illustrated by the *Griefield* case, if an overhanging limb of a tree planted by a landowner or his predecessor falls on an adjoining landowner's house during a storm, there will be liability for the resulting damage. However, if this same tree was of natural growth as defined by the Restatement, Torts Section 840, the landowner will not be held liable for damage.

A different issue concerning the liability of a landowner is found to exist in relation to a tree growing on one's land which is blown down upon the premises of another causing injury but which does not overhang upon the adjoining landowner's premises. An old principal of law under these circumstances was set forth in the case of *Sheldon v. Sherman*.[11] In *Sheldon*, the plaintiff brought an action against the defendant alleging that the defendant's logs had drifted down the Hudson River upon his land, remaining there a considerable time, causing great loss and damage. The Court in deciding upon various issues in the case laid down a rule of law which has remained in effect to this day. The Court stated that if a tree growing upon the land of one is blown down upon the premises of another, and in its fall injures another's shrubbery, house, or person, such individual has no redress against the person upon whose land the tree grew. The Court in Sheldon premised its holding upon the fact that the injury arises from an unfortuitous occurrence beyond the control of man. The Court labeled the occurrence as being "the act of God".[12]

Is a landowner liable for damages caused by an act of God?

Typically, a landowner will not be held liable for damages caused by an act of God. However, in order to understand under what circumstances a landowner will not be held liable for damages caused by a tree falling as a result of an act of God, it is necessary to determine precisely what constitutes an act of God. A case which sets forth an excellent definition of an act of God is *Gulf Oil Corporation v. Lemmons*.[13] In the *Gulf Oil Corporation* case, an action was brought by the plaintiff against the defendant for damage to growing crops caused by oil which escaped from the defendant's pond when flood waters extended over the defendant's property.

The Court in construing the definition of an act of God ruled that it is the general view that an act of God represents some inevitable accident which could not have been prevented by human care, skill and foresight, but which results exclusively from nature's cause, such as lightning, tempest and floods.[14]

A case similar to the *Gulf Oil Corporation* case is *Buschelberg v. Chicago, Burlington and Quincy R. Co.*[15] In the *Buschelberg* case, an action was brought by the plaintiff for damages to the plaintiff's land by flood waters flowing through an underpass in the defendant railroad company's right-of-way embankment. The Court in deciding upon the definition of an act of God ruled that an act of God is an occurrence due to natural causes which could not be prevented by ordinary skill and foresight.[16]

It is apparent that the common thread running through those cases dealing with the definition of an act of God is that an act of God must be one stemming from totally natural causes which could not be prevented against through the actions of any particular individual. An analysis of the foregoing cases cited providing various definitions of an act of God discloses that there is a requirement of the entire exclusion of human agency from the cause of the injury or loss. As a result, where an intervening human agency contributes to cause damage, such damage cannot be said to have been caused by an act of God. An injury will not be considered an act of God if it results from or is contributed to by human activities which may have been prevented by the exercise of reasonable diligence or ordinary care.

A landowner will not escape liability for damages caused by an unsound or defective tree located on the landowner's property. For example, in *Gibson v. Denton*,[17] the plaintiff brought an action against the defendant for damages caused by a decayed tree located on the defendant's property which fell on the plaintiff's house during a gale. The defendant in *Gibson* alleged that the fall of the tree was caused by an extra-ordinary wind or gale, which could not have been anticipated and, therefore, the defendant was not liable.

The Court in *Gibson* held that if a tree growing upon the land of an individual is blown down upon the premises of another, and in its fall injures his shrubbery or his house or his person, he has no redress against the person upon whose land the tree grew.[18] The Court in *Gibson* stated: "But it does not appear that the learned judge was speaking of an unsound tree standing on premises of a party near the house of his neighbor, liable, in any high wind to fall upon it, and which the owner of the tree, after notice of its condition, neglected to remove it."[19] The Court in its holding seemed to be following the principle that an injury will not be viewed as an act of God if it could have been prevented by the exercise of reasonable diligence or ordinary care. Since the tree could have been removed by the defendant preventing the injury complained of, it did not matter that the tree was blown over by an act of nature.

A similar case which illustrates the principle that an injury caused by a tree will result in liability and will not be considered an act of God if it results from or is contributed to by human agency is the case of *Short v. Kerr.*[20] In *Short*, an action was brought as a result of an accident occurring when a tree which a foreman and his gang were excavating fell the wrong way because of a great puff of wind resulting in the death of the foreman. The defendant in *Short* alleged that he was not liable for the damage caused because the accident resulting in the foreman's death was caused through an act of God and the employer was not liable for such acts.

The Court in determining whether or not the defendant was entitled to the act-of-God defense, and therefore, absolved from liability stated: "The phrase has been otherwise defined an act, event, happening, or occurrence, a disaster, an effect due to natural causes, an inevitable accident or disaster, or natural and inevitable necessity which implies entire exclusion of all human agency, which operates without interference or aid from man, and which results from natural causes and is in no sense attributable to human agency; an accident which could not have been occasioned by human agency but proceeds from physical causes alone."[21] The Court ruled that from the facts as disclosed by the evidence, the tree fell as a result of acts caused by human agency; and, therefore, the defendant was not entitled to the act-of-God defense.[22]

The principle of law arising out of all of these cases concerning the liability of a landowner for damages caused as a result of a tree falling on an adjoining landowner's property or, for that matter, injury caused to anyone, is that a landowner will not be responsible for those injuries strictly arising out of an act of God. However, if the injury caused by the falling tree could have been prevented by reasonable diligence or ordinary care or was an injury contributed to by human agency, the landowner will not be entitled to the act-of-God defense, and will be liable for all injuries sustained as a result of the falling tree.

Chapter 2

Recreational User Statutes— A Deviation From the Norm Concerning a Landowner's Duty With Regard to Premises Liability

The preceding section made clear the duty of care owed by a landowner to others with regard to trees growing on the landowner's property. A landowner is not only held to the duty of common prudence in maintaining trees on the landowner's property, but the landowner is also held to an even greater duty of inspection to discover possible defective conditions of a tree in order to prevent the tree from falling and injuring others. The law in this area appears to be straight forward and is in accord with basic principles of negligence with regard to premises liability.

However, it is very important to be aware of the divergence which exists in the area of premises liability as a result of recreational use statutes which have been enacted by certain states.

What is a recreational use statute?

In general, recreational use statutes exempt a landowner from liability for injuries which occur to a recreational user of the landowner's property.

What affect does a recreational use statute have on a landowner's duty in the maintenance of the landowner's property?

A detailed analysis of the definition of a recreational use statute along with an overview of its application under various fact situations will provide some insight as to the effect which a recreational use statute has concerning a landowner's duty with regard to premises liability.

A typical recreational use statute can be found in use by the State of Ohio. Ohio Revised Code Section 1533.181 entitled, Exemptions From Liability To Recreational Users, states in full:

(A) No owner, lessee, or occupant of premises:

(1) Owes any duty to a recreational user to keep the premises safe for entry or use;

(2) Extends any assurance to a recreational user, through the act of giving permission, that the premises are safe for entry or use;

(3) Assumes responsibility for or incurs liability for any injury to a person or property caused by any act of a recreational user.

Ohio Revised Code Section 1533.18 provides the definitions as to that which will be considered a premises and recreational user in order to fall within the parameters of the recreational use statute and reads in full:

(A) "Premises" means all privately-owned lands, ways, waters, and any buildings and structures thereon, and all state-owned lands, ways, and waters leased to a private person, firm, organization, or corporation, including any buildings and structures thereon.

(B) "Recreational user" means a person to whom permission has been granted, without the payment of a fee or consideration to the owner, lessee, or occupant of premises, other than a fee or consideration paid to the State or any agency thereof, to enter upon premises to hunt, fish, trap, camp, hike, swim, or engage in other recreational pursuits.

Are govern-ment agencies affected by recreational use statutes?

Yes, as can be readily seen in reading the recreational use statute enacted in Ohio, an owner, lessee or occupant of premises as defined refers not only to private individuals but to governmental agencies as well.

Under what circumstances is an individual considered to be a recreational user?

A review of the facts which have taken place in a particular case in comparison with a state's recreational use statute is really the only way to determine if an individual is actually a recreational user for the purposes of determining the issue of liability and duty owed by a landowner. An excellent case which analyzes the recreational use statute and its application is *Moss v. Department of Natural Resources.*[23] In *Moss*, the plaintiff brought suit against the state for a fractured ankle she sustained as a result of stepping into a hole which she alleged was caused by the combined negligence of the state and other private parties. The plaintiff further alleged that she had made certain purchases at the park where she was injured which would cause her to fall outside the reach of the recreational use statute.

The first issue the Court was called upon to decide in *Moss* was whether state-owned lands were premises within the recreational use statute granting an owner, lessor or occupier of a premises immunity from suit by a recreational user. In deciding upon the issues, the Court in *Moss* recognized the fact that the state had in the past waived its immunity from liability and consented to be sued, and have its liability determined in accordance with the same rules of law applicable to suits between private parties. The Court further recognized the fact that one such rule of law applicable to private parties was Ohio Revised Code Section 1533.181(A), otherwise known as the recreational use statute and, therefore, the same rule of law was applicable to state-owned lands as it was to privately-owned property.[24]

Does it matter if an individual pays a fee to be on the property for a recreational purpose?

The Court in the *Moss* case was called upon to decide the issue of whether or not an individual will still be considered a recreational user for purposes of the recreational use statute when some sort of fee or consideration is paid by the individual. As previously stated, the plaintiff in *Moss* alleged that she could not be considered a recreational user under the statute and further barred from bringing suit due to the fact that she had made certain purchases at the park. The plaintiff based her assertion on the fact that the statutory definition of "recreational user" is one who enters a premises for recreational pursuits without paying an admittance charge other than a fee or consideration paid to the state or any agency thereof. She further alleged that the purchases she made constituted the payment of a fee or consideration under the statute and that it was not necessary that an entrance or admittance fee be paid at the park for one to fall outside the recreational user status.[25]

The Court in deciding upon this issue ruled that the phrase, "other than a fee or consideration paid to the state or any agency thereof," makes reference to license fees or other privileges secured from the state for the purpose of engaging in recreational pursuits. In further ruling upon what is defined as consideration under the recreational use statute, the Court decided that consideration shall not be deemed given unless it is a charge necessary to utilize the overall benefits of a recreational area so that it may be regarded as an entrance or admittance fee.[26] The Court's opinion in *Moss* seems to indicate that the definition of consideration is applicable to both private-owned lands as well as state-owned lands.

As noted, ordinarily a landowner will be held to a duty of common prudence in the maintenance of the landowner's property. However, the typical recreational use statute provides a divergence from general principles concerning a landowner's normal standard and duty of care and further relieves a landowner from any duty of care owed to a recreational user.

What is a recreational activity?

An excellent analysis as to what will be considered a recreational activity under the language of a recreational use statute can be found in the case of *Fetherolf v. State, Department of Natural Resources.*[27] In *Fetherolf*, the plaintiff sought damages for injuries to his right leg, ankle and foot as a result of a fall during a visit with his family to a state park. The plaintiff alleged he sustained his injuries as a result of his stepping onto a muddy area which was negligently maintained. The plaintiff further alleged that the state was guilty of willful and wanton misconduct in that there was a duty to warn him of the dangerous situation which existed.[28]

The Court in *Fetherolf* was confronted with two very important issues. The first being whether the plaintiff could be considered a recreational user for the purposes of the statute when his only use of the park was in sitting on the beach and watching other members of his family swim. The second issue involved the duty of care, if any, which was owed to a recreational user in the case of a premises being used for recreational purposes.

In deciding upon whether the plaintiff was engaged in a recreational pursuit at the time of his injuries, the Court in *Fetherolf* ruled that sitting on the beach watching others swim constitutes a recreational activity within the contemplation of the recreational use statute. The Court further ruled that a recreational pursuit need not be specifically delineated in the recreational use statute and that sitting on the beach or otherwise close to the water is a recreational pursuit associated with swimming.[29]

In deciding upon the second issue as to what, if any, duty is owed to a recreational user by a premises owner, the Court in *Fetherolf* ruled that an owner of premises owes no duty to a recreational user to keep a premises safe for entry or use and, furthermore, that an action cannot be brought against an owner by a recreational user for alleged wanton misconduct.[30]

While the *Fetherolf* case is important in showing that there is absolutely no duty of care owed to a recreational user by a premises owner, it also helps illustrate the lengths that the courts will go in order to make the determination that an individual is a recreational user thereby absolving a premises owner from liability.

What is the underlying purpose of a recreational use statute?

The reason that the courts seem to go to such great lengths in finding an individual to be a recreational user thereby falling within the parameters of the recreational use statute can be best explained by looking to the underlying purpose of the statute. A case which provides insight as to the underlying purpose of a recreational use statute is *Marrik v. Cleveland Metropark Board of Commissioners.*[31] *Marrik* involves a situation wherein a plaintiff brought suit against the state based upon injuries she received while sledding in a park.

After making a finding that the plaintiff was, in fact, a recreational user for purposes of exempting the state from liability under the statute, the Court in *Marrik* provided insight as to the purpose and intent of the recreational use statute. The Court in *Marrik* stated that statutory immunity for landowners under the recreational use statute promotes the development and availability of property for recreational use. The Court further stated that it is the purpose of the statute to encourage owners of premises suitable for recreational pursuits to open their land to public use without worry about liability.[32]

Presently, more than half of the states now have laws similar to the recreational use statute of Ohio, however, they vary in degree of their effect and application. It is clear from the Ohio cases discussed that the Ohio recreational use statute provides for total exemption of liability to a premises owner to those who clearly meet the definition of a recreational user.

Do all recreational use statutes exempt a landowner from liability for injuries sustained on the landowner's property?

No, it is important to note that there are states that have recreational use statutes which do not completely insulate a premises owner from liability to recreational users and, in some instances, will hold a premises owner liable for injuries caused to a recreational user while on the premises owner's property for recreational purposes. One such state that provides an excellent illustration of a recreational use statute which does not provide for complete exemption from liability to a premises owner for injuries to a recreational user is the State of Alabama.

Alabama's recreational use statute is contained in the Code of Alabama 1975, Sc 35-15-1 et seq. and governs the duty of care owed by an owner of a premises to persons on the landowner's premises for recreational purposes. The statute states in part:

> Section 1. An owner, lessee, or occupant of premises owes no duty of care to keep such premises safe for entry and use by others for

hunting, fishing, trapping, camping, water sports, hiking, boating, sight-seeing, or other recreational purposes, or to give any warning of hazardous conditions, use of structures or activities on such premises to persons entering for the above-stated purposes, except as provided in Section 3 of this Act.

Section 2. An owner, lessee, or occupant of premises who gives permission to another to hunt, fish, trap, camp, hike, sight-see, or engage in other sporting or recreational activities upon such premises, does not thereby (a) extend any assurance that the premises are safe for such purpose; (b) constitute the person to whom permission has been granted the legal status of an invitee to whom a duty of care is owed; or (c) assume responsibility for or incur liability for any injury to person or property caused by an act of such person to whom permission has been granted, except as provided in Section 3 of this Act.

Section 3. This Act does not limit the liability which otherwise exists (a) for willful or malicious failure to guard or warn against a dangerous condition, use, structure or activity; or (b) for injury suffered in any case where permission to hunt, fish, trap, camp, hike or sight-see was granted for commercial enterprise for profit; or (c) for injury caused by acts of persons to whom permission to hunt, fish, trap, camp, hike or sight-see was granted to third persons as to whom the person granting permission, or the owner, leasee or occupant of the premises, owed a duty to keep the premises safe or to warn of danger.

Section 4. Nothing in this Act creates a duty of care or ground of liability for injury to person or property.

Section 5. Nothing in this Act shall be construed as granting or creating a right for any person to go on the lands of another without permission of the landowner.

A case which illustrates the application and effect of the Alabama version of the recreation use statute is *Driskill v. Alabama Power Co.*[33] In *Driskill*, a boater brought an action against a power company for injuries sustained when the motorboat he was operating on the company's lake ran into a submerged tree trunk. In bringing the action, the boater alleged negligence and wanton conduct by the power company in causing or allowing a submerged tree trunk to exist in a manner which was hidden from view, and in failing to mark it and warn the boater of its danger.[34]

The Court in *Driskill* based its decision on the construction of the Alabama recreational use statute. In making its decision, the Court recognized that the recreational use statute was intended to insure that landowners were not to be held to a standard of due care toward persons upon their land with permission for recreational purposes. The Court further held that the duty owed to a recreational user was that duty which is owed to a licensee.[35]

In construing the duty of care owed by a premises owner to a recreational user or licensee, the Court in *Driskill* noted that a premises owner will generally owe no duty to warn a licensee of a potentially dangerous condition unless the landowner does some positive act which creates a new hidden danger, pitfall or trap, which is a condition that a person could not avoid by the use of reasonable care and skill. The Court further stated that a recreational user/licensee's entrance on the land carries with it no right to expect the land to be made safe for that individual's reception, but the recreational user must assume the risk of whatever may be encountered. The Court, however, did note that a landowner will be held liable if the landowner does some act which goes beyond mere negligence.[36]

In making its decision as to whether the power company was liable to the boater while occupying the status of a recreational user, the Court in *Driskill* carefully reviewed the facts which had transpired. Evidence showed that a row of trees growing in the water had rotted and fallen into the power company's lake over a period of time and that their stumps had been left to remain. The power company reduced the water level of the lake in the fall and winter, revealing the stumps, but would begin to raise the water level in the month of March so that in the summer months, when water sports were popular, the stumps would be invisible.[37]

Upon consideration of the facts, the Court in *Driskill* found there to be evidence that from the time the lake was built the power company did nothing except raise and lower the water for the power company's purposes. The Court found this not to be a positive act which created a new hidden danger, trap or pitfall, thereby, holding that the power company was not liable to the boater for his injuries while a recreational user on the power company's premises.[38]

In reviewing the area of law regarding recreational use statutes, it is important to know the particular extent of immunity from liability that a particular recreational use statute will provide to a premises owner when a recreational user is injured on the premises owner's property. Certain recreational use statutes provide that there is no duty owed by a premises owner to a recreational user, such as that found in Ohio, while others will provide that a duty exists in the same form as that owed to a licensee by a premises owner such as that found in Alabama where liability exists for positive acts creating new dangers by premises' owners. Therefore, a review of each state's particular recreational use statute is necessary in order to determine the nature and extent of liability which a premises owner may have with regard to a recreational user utilizing the benefits of the premises owner's property.

The recreational use statutes are important in their exemption to a premises owner from liability resulting from injuries sustained by a recreational user on the premises owner's property. The recreational use statutes are also important in their effect on a premises owner's duty of care with regard to trees growing on the premises owner's property. Even though, in certain instances, a premises owner owes no duty of care with regard to the maintenance of trees on the premises to a recreational user as defined in certain recreational use statutes, a duty of common prudence in maintaining trees on one's property still exists and is owed to one who is not a recreational user. It is very important for the premises owner to realize the significance of this point inasmuch as a premises owner is unable to choose in advance the status of a particular individual who might possibly be injured on the premises owner's property. Therefore, in order to prevent costly and needless litigation, the intelligent premises owner should always take measures in maintaining the trees located on the premises in a prudent manner.

Chapter 3

Rights and Liabilities of Adjoining Landowners as to Trees Growing on Boundary Line

The courts have been faced with various issues concerning adjoining landowners and trees on their property. One such issue relates to the rights and liabilities of adjoining landowners as to trees growing on their common boundary line.

Who is the owner of a boundary line tree?

A tree which is located on the common boundary line of adjoining landowners is owned by both landowners as tenants in common. The courts have generally taken the position that trees standing on the boundary line between adjoining landowners are owned jointly by both landowners. The courts have also held that trees are jointly owned by adjoining landowners when the trees are treated by the adjoining landowners as their common property pursuant to an agreement or a course of conduct.

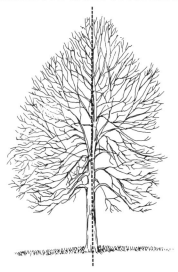

A case which supports the proposition that a tree growing on the boundary line between adjoining landowners generally belongs to the landowners jointly or as tenants in common is *Scarborough v. Wooldhill*.[39] In *Scarborough*, the plaintiff and defendant owned adjoining orange orchards which were separated by a row of Cypress trees growing on the boundary line between their properties. The defendant cut down eight of these trees, and threatened to continue to cut every alternate two trees until he had cut one-half of the entire row. The plaintiff brought suit against the defendant and the trial court rendered judgment in favor of the plaintiff and perpetually enjoined the defendant from cutting down, injuring or destroying any of the remaining trees growing on the boundary line.

The Court in deciding upon the issue of ownership of the boundary line trees ruled that if the tree stands so nearly upon the dividing line between the lands that portions of its body extend into each, the tree is the property, in common, of both landowners.

What rights do the owners of a boundary line tree have in the cutting or trimming of a boundary line tree?

The Court in *Scarborough* set forth the rights that owners of a boundary line tree have in cutting or trimming such a tree and held that neither of the property owners is at liberty to cut the tree without the consent of the other, nor to cut away the part which extends into the property owner's land, if injury would result to the common property in the tree. In defining the type of ownership existing in the boundary line trees, the Court ruled that the defendant's estate in the row of cypress trees must be considered merely as that of a tenant in common in the trees themselves, with an easement upon the plaintiff's land for the sustenance of such trees.[40]

In *Robinson v. Clapp*,[41] a Maple tree of about forty years' growth, about sixteen inches in diameter and a branch extension of from forty to fifty feet stood on the boundary line between the premises of the plaintiff and the defendant. A question arose as to the defendant's right to remove the tree or parts of the tree. In construing the rights and liabilities of the adjoining landowners in relation to the boundary line tree, the Court ruled that in such a situation, each of the landowners upon whose land any part of a trunk of a tree stands has an interest in that tree, a property in it, equal, in the first instance to or, perhaps, rather identical with, the part which is upon the property owner's land.[42] Simply speaking, the Court was holding that the adjoining property owners held a common interest in the tree standing on the common boundary of the landowners.

Can a tree located solely on the property of an adjoining landowner be considered to be a boundary line tree?

Yes, a tree growing between landowners' property has also been recognized to be the common property of adjoining landowners when they have treated it as common property by express agreement or by their course of conduct and the tree is actually located completely on one of the landowner's property. For example, in *Rhoding v. Keck*,[43] the plaintiffs filed suit against the defendant alleging malicious and wanton destruction of four trees which allegedly grew on the boundary line between plaintiffs' and defendant's property. The defendant admitted removing the trees but alleged that they were completely on his property and that he had the right to destroy them. The plaintiffs, on the other hand, contended they were tenants in common of the trees with the defendant. The Court ruled upon the issue as to whether the plaintiffs and the defendant were, in fact, tenants in common of the trees. The

Court held that a test in determining whether trees are boundary line trees and thereby entitled to protection is whether they were planted jointly, or jointly cared for, or were treated as a partition between adjoining properties.

A case relied upon by the Court in *Rhoding* is *Weisel v. Hobbs.*[44] In *Weisel*, the plaintiff sought by injunction to restrain the defendants from cutting down a large ornamental shade tree. The Trial Court found for the defendants ruling that the tree was entirely upon the real estate of the defendants. On appeal, the Court in *Weisel* held that where the trunk of a tree impinges upon the lot line, and where the respective owners have for years jointly cared for the tree and divided the expenses of protecting it from the ravages of time and the elements, each owner has an interest in the tree sufficient to demand that the owner of the other portion shall not destroy the tree.[45]

A final case dealing with the recognition of a boundary line tree as common property as a result of an agreement or course of conduct by adjoining landowners is *Robins v. Roberts.*[46] In *Robins*, the plaintiff brought an action to restrain the defendant from maintaining a row of Willow trees along the boundary common to the plaintiff's land and the defendant's land, and from permitting the roots and branches of the trees to extend into and over the plaintiff's land. The defendant's defense to the cause of action was that the row of trees in question marked the common boundary line between the plaintiff's and the defendant's two properties and that the trees were, and for forty years had been, maintained by the parties as a common boundary line fence.

The Court in *Robins* ruled that trees standing on boundary lines between adjoining owners are common property of both owners who are tenants in common as to the trees. The Court further held that there was sufficient evidence to support a finding that the trees planted on the land between the properties of the plaintiff and the defendant for more than thirty-five years had served as a boundary fence with the acquiescence of both owners.[47]

It is apparent from the cases cited that the courts will protect the interests of an adjoining landowner with regard to a tree standing on the boundary line of the adjoining properties under a variety of different circumstances. In certain situations, courts will protect the interests of an adjoining landowner as a tenant in common when there is a tree standing on the border line between the adjoining owners when that border line passes through the trunk or body of the tree above the surface of the soil. In another instance, the courts will protect the interests of an adjoining landowner as a tenant in common when there is a tree or group of trees which both adjoining landowners recognize as being a common boundary line regardless of whether or not it is truly the actual boundary line.

There seems to be a common sense rationale behind the decisions of the courts on this issue. If the courts were to hold that each adjoining landowner is the absolute owner of that part of the tree standing on each individual's property, it would lead to a division in the tree that when cut by one owner would lead to devastating results. It would give the right to one adjoining landowner to cut down that part of the tree growing on that landowner's property, thereby destroying that part of the tree belonging to the other property owner.

Under what circumstances can a landowner remove a boundary line tree?

While it is true that the courts have generally found that a boundary line tree is the common property of both abutting landowners, the courts have also been confronted with the question as to what rights each adjoining landowner has in reference to those boundary line trees. One such issue that the courts are confronted with is an adjoining owner's right to completely remove or destroy a boundary line tree. The law regarding the rights of ownership of a boundary line tree whose trunk lies partly upon the lands of different owners was set forth in the case of *Doran v. Rugg*.[48] In *Doran*, the plaintiffs and the defendant were adjoining owners of real estate along whose common bound ran a line of tall White Pine trees. An action for damages was brought by the plaintiffs against the defendant as a result of the defendant's actions in cutting down several of the trees standing on the common boundary line.

In determining the rights each landowner had with regard to the boundary line trees, the Court held that each landowner upon whose land any part of a trunk of a tree stands has an interest in that tree, which embraces the right to demand that the owner of the other portion shall only use his part so as not to unreasonably injure or destroy the whole.[49] The *Luke* case involved an action for damages arising out of the defendant's cutting down of two trees growing on the boundary line of the defendant's and plaintiff's land. The Court in Luke noted that if the trees were on the boundary line separating the two properties, the defendant and the plaintiff would be joint owners of the trees, and neither of them would have the right to cut or injure the trees without the consent of the other.[50]

Even though neither adjoining landowner has the right to remove, injure or destroy a boundary line tree without the consent of the adjoining landowner, both landowners are obligated to use their property in a reasonable way.

For example, a case which dealt with an abutting landowner's right to use his property in a reasonable way to the detriment of a tree growing on the common boundary line is *Higdon v. Henderson*.[51] In *Higdon*, an action was brought between adjoining landowners whereby the plaintiffs sought to recover damages for the destruction by the defendant of a tree growing on the common boundary line. The plaintiffs alleged in their petition that there was located on the lot line between the adjoining properties of the plaintiffs and defendant a large towering Oak tree, and that defendant while constructing a residence on his lot adjacent to the plaintiffs', made an excavation on the defendant's side of the property which cut open and exposed the roots of the tree resulting in the death of the tree.

The Court in *Higdon* recognized that generally one of two adjoining landowners has no right to damage or destroy a tree on the boundary line without the consent or permission of the other adjoining landowner, but, that the rule is qualified by the right of an abutting owner to use such property in a reasonable way. The Court found that the facts presented in the case by the plaintiffs were not sufficient to constitute a cause of action for damages, because the plaintiffs did not show an unreasonable use by the defendant of his property. The Court ruled that the allegations showed that the defendant was excavating on his own lot to build a residence and nothing more, which was not an unreasonable use of the defendant's property.[52]

Conversely, an example of a case which dealt with an adjoining landowner's right to cut down a tree growing on the boundary line when there exists a threat of damages which would result from the boundary line tree is *Lemon v. Curington*.[53] In *Lemon*, an action was brought between adjoining landowners wherein the plaintiff sought to remove, as a nuisance, trees planted on the common boundary line by the defendant's predecessors in interest. There had been planted two Poplar trees on the common boundary line. Reviewing the facts, the Court further found that the trunks of the trees had extended upon the plaintiff's property a distance of two or more feet and four to five feet from the plaintiff's house. It was also found that the branches of the trees had a spread of approximately thirty feet and extended over the plaintiff's property. Of critical importance to the Court was the fact that the roots of one of these boundary line trees extended from the boundary line to the foundation of the plaintiff's house exerting pressure against the foundation causing the basement to crack and the wall of the plaintiff's house to move inward.

In deciding upon the issue of whether or not the plaintiff should be given the authority to remove the offending trees, the Court ruled that while there is some conflict of authority relating to this issue, it is generally held that where actual damage has been sustained and is likely to continue, the injured landowner may maintain an action for the abatement of the nuisance. The Court affirmed the lower court's decision in authorizing the destruction of one of the Poplar trees which caused the damages complained of. However, it is important to note that both courts failed to allow the plaintiff the right to move the other Poplar tree based on the finding that the removal of this tree was not necessary for the protection of the plaintiff's property.[54]

What right does an adjoining landowner have to cut or trim branches and roots of a boundary line tree which transgress on to the landowner's property?

The courts have also been confronted with the issue concerning the rights of adjoining land owners to trim or cut trees which are growing on the boundary lines of their properties. It seems that the right of one adjoining landowner to trim or cut off the limbs or branches of boundary line trees is allowed within certain limitations dictated by the facts of each case. For example, in the case of *Grandona v. Loodal*,[55] trees that had originally been planted on the defendant's land grew so large that the trunks of the trees and their branches extended over into the plaintiff's property. The Court in *Grandona* ruled that so far as the trees and overhanging branches of the trees were on or over the plaintiff's land, they belonged to him and he could have cut them off or trimmed them as he chose.[56]

However, this right to trim boundary line trees as mentioned in the *Grandona* case has been qualified in the case of *Robinson v. Clapp*.[57] In *Robinson*, a Maple tree of about forty years' growth, about sixteen inches in diameter and with a branch extension of from forty to fifty feet stood on the boundary line between the premises of the plaintiff and the defendant. The issue arose as to the defendant's right to remove the tree or, in the alternative, parts of the tree.

In deciding on this issue, the Court ruled that a tree which stands upon the dividing line between lands where portions of its body extend into each, the same is the property in common of the landowners. The Court in *Robinson* ruled that neither of the landowners is at liberty to cut the tree without the consent of the other, nor to cut away the part which extends into his land, if he thereby injures the common property of the tree.[58]

It does not appear that there exists a great deal of authority on the subject relating to an abutting landowner's right to trim or cut off limbs or branches of a tree growing on a common boundary line. However, the authority that does exist seems to suggest that generally where roots and branches of trees standing on the boundary line extend over or into the adjoining land, the owner of the land may cut them off up to the trunk of the tree so long as the landowner does not injure the tree. However, the right of the abutting landowner to have boundary line trees protected from injury will be balanced against the right of an adjoining landowner to use such property in a reasonable manner.

Who is responsible for the care and maintenance of a boundary line tree?

With respect to a boundary line tree either as a result of the location of the tree in proximity to the property lines or through the course of conduct existing between adjoining landowners, it is generally recognized that both owners of the tree are equally responsible for the care and maintenance of the tree. Both adjoining landowners are legally responsible for the cost of necessary maintenance to the tree and both owe the same duty of care that an individual has with regard to any tree which is located on the landowner's property. Furthermore, the co-owners' of a boundary line tree are jointly and severally liable for any injuries caused through their joint negligence in failing to properly care for a boundary line tree growing at or near the boundary lines of their property.

Chapter 4
Rights and Liabilities of Adjoining Landowners as to Trees not Growing on Boundary Line

A somewhat different issue exists regarding the rights an adjoining landowner has in relation to trees growing on a neighbor's property which are not boundary line trees.

What right does a landowner have when a neighbor's tree limb hangs over the landowner's property?

It is generally held that when a neighboring landowner's tree limb hangs over an adjoining landowner's property, the adjoining property owner has an absolute right to cut the tree limbs off the tree up to the property line. For example, in *Murray v. Heabron*,[59] the plaintiff brought a cause of action against the defendant for declaratory judgment as to the rights of adjoining landowners arising as a result of limbs and branches of a tree protruding over a property line.

The Court in deciding upon the rights of the plaintiff ruled that a landowner's property

rights extend indefinitely upward, and those rights are protected from invasion by an adjoining landowner to the same extent as surface rights.

Does a landowner have the right to take the law into his own hands and remove a neighbor's tree limb which overhangs upon the landowner's property?

Yes, the Court in *Murray* set forth the common law view as to the landowner's right to remove overhanging limbs from a neighbor's trees holding that an owner of land has the right to cut off, sever or eliminate in any manner the owner finds expedient any portion of a tree which protrudes or overhangs in or upon the landowner's property.[60]

A case similar to *Murray* is *Bonde v. Bishop*.[61] In *Bonde*, an action was brought by the plaintiff against the defendants for a declaration that the defendants' tree overhanging the plaintiff's premises was a nuisance. The Court in *Bonde* ruled that to the extent that limbs or roots of a tree extend upon an adjoining landowner's property, the latter may remove them but only to the boundary line.[62] The Court in *Bonde* also held that while it is the absolute right of a landowner to remove those portions of trees which encroach on the property owner's land whether they cause damage or not, it is rather anomalous that to obtain court help in the matter he must first prove that the encroachment constitutes a nuisance. The Court recognized the fact that a landowner, merely because the landowner does not desire a neighbor's tree to overhang the landowner's premises, can, in a sense, take the law into the landowner's own hands and cut off the encroachment, but, to act in what is probably a more orderly manner and apply to the court for an injunction restraining the tree owner from allowing the tree to encroach, the landowner has to prove the encroachment constitutes a nuisance.[63]

To what extent is the landowner entitled to trim back the limbs and roots of an adjoining neighbor's tree?

A landowner is entitled to trim both limbs and roots which intrude onto the landowner's property up to the property line. For example, in *Michalson v. Nutting*,[64] the plaintiffs brought suit alleging that roots from a Poplar tree growing upon the land of the defendants had penetrated the plaintiff's land and had filled up sewer and drain pipes resulting in damage. The Court in *Michalson* ruled that a property owner may cut off boughs and roots of a neighbor's trees which intrude into the property owner's land.[65]

In *Gostina v. Ryland*,[66] the plaintiff brought a suit to have overhanging branches of trees and shrubs of the defendant removed from his property. In deciding upon the right of the plaintiff to compel removal, the Court in *Gostina* ruled that it has been a principle of law that the landowner has the exclusive right to the space above the surface of the landowner's property.[67] The Court further stated that on the same principle it is held that the branches of trees extending over adjoining land constitute a nuisance—at least in the sense that the owner of the land encroached upon may himself cut off the offending growth. The Court also held that a property owner may, without notice, if the property owner has not encouraged the maintenance of the nuisance, and, after notice if the property owner has, clip the branches of trees standing on adjoining property which overhang the property owner's premises.[68]

What surface and subsurface rights does a landowner have with regard to the landowner's property?

The law is very clear as to what rights an adjoining landowner has when a neighbor's tree limbs or roots hang over or encroach upon the landowner's property. The adjoining property owner has an absolute right to cut those parts of the tree which encroach upon the landowner's property. It is recognized that a landowner owns both the ground below and the air above such property, and the landowner has a right to protect it.

Are the surface rights to a landowner's property qualified in any manner?

Yes. There are some jurisdictions which are placing restrictions on a landowner's right to erect structures or plant trees which might interfere with an adjoining landowner's access to light or view. As a general rule, a landowner has no natural right to air, light or an unobstructed view and the law is reluctant to imply such a right.[69] However, it has been held that such a right may be created by private parties through the granting of an easement or through the adoption of conditions, covenants and restrictions or by the legislature as by creating a right to sunlight for solar collectors.[70] Also, local governments may protect views and provide for light and air through the adoption of height limits.[71]

The case of *Pacifica Homeowners' Assn.* dealt with many of the issues regarding adjoining landowners' rights to air, light and view. *Pacifica Homeowners' Assn.* involved an action by members of a homeowners' association to enjoin a retirement community from allowing trees on its property to grow higher than the retirement community's five-story building, contending that the retirement community's property was burdened with a servitude in favor of the homeowners' association not to permit any obstruction exceeding the height of the five-story building. The association contended that the conditional use permit granted the retirement community intended to give the association a right to an unobstructed view. The homeowners' association consisted of single-family residences with views of the ocean. Covenants contained in the homeowners' deeds protected those views from future obstruction.[72]

The retirement community was granted a conditional use permit by the City in 1958 which restricted the construction of any structures on the property to a height of five floors. By 1984, Eucalyptus and Pine trees on the retirement community property exceeded the height of its five-story building and were obstructing the views of the homeowners' association residences.[73]

The homeowners' association brought suit alleging that the retirement community had a duty under the conditional use permit to maintain its land so as not to be injurious to the association's property and that the retirement community was creating a nuisance by allowing its trees to obstruct the association's light and view.

The Court in the *Pacifica Homeowners' Assn.* recognized that a landowner ordinarily has no natural right to air, light, or an unobstructed view unless created by the private parties through the granting of an easement or through the adoption of conditions, covenants and restrictions. The Court also recognized instances whereby the Legislature can create a right to sunlight for solar collectors citing California's Public Resources Code Section 25980, otherwise referred to as "The Solar Shade Control Act of 1979," which prohibits shading of solar collectors that results from tree growth after a solar collector is installed. The Court also recognized that local governments can create rights to air and light in their adoption of height limits.[74]

After making these recognitions, the Court in *Pacifica* held that the requirement of a conditional use permit that the developer obtain the planning commissioner's approval of a landscape plan, and the commissioner's approval of the plan, did not establish the existence of a height limit on trees. The Court further held that it must be inferred that the planning commission approved the mature height of the trees since the commission attached no trimming or height restrictions on the trees.[75]

As can be seem from the *Pacifica* case, the property owner and/or landscape architect must be familiar with any easements, covenants or restrictions which pertain to the property as to obstructions to air, light and view which may run in favor of the adjoining landowner's property. Furthermore, the landowner and/or landscape architect must be familiar with any applicable legislative acts, such as "The Solar Shade Control Act," or any local government ordinances pertaining to height restrictions which may place limitations on the height of trees.

Chapter 5

Liability for Injuries or Damage Resulting From a Falling Tree or Limb Abutting a Street or Highway

Who is liable for damages caused by a tree abutting a street or highway?

Another issue that frequently comes before the courts is who is liable for injuries caused by a falling tree abutting a street or highway. In many cases, it has been held that a municipality will be liable for damages caused by the fall of a tree or a limb of a tree abutting a street or highway if the municipality had notice, or should have had notice that the tree posed a threat of danger. For example, in *Wershba v. Lynn*,[76] the plaintiff brought a cause of action in tort against the city for personal injuries sustained by him when a public shade tree located on a public way fell on an automobile in which he was an occupant.

In determining whether the city was liable for the damages caused by the fallen tree, the Court found that the plaintiff was injured by reason of a defect in or upon a way which might have been remedied by reasonable care and diligence on

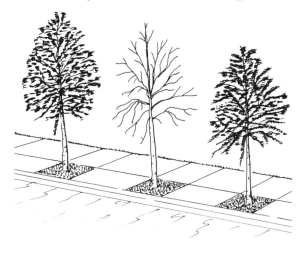

the part of the defendant. The Court in *Wershba* held that a shade tree within the limits of a highway may, because of its decayed or unsound condition, be a defect. Based on the facts presented in the case, the Court found that the defect which caused the accident had been in existence for a period of time sufficient to constitute a reasonable notice to the defendant. It appears that from the Court's holding in *Wershba* a city will only be liable if it fails to live up to a reasonable man standard commonly used in determining liability in negligence cases.[77]

Under what circumstances are governmental agencies immune from liability?

There are some instances in which the courts have taken the view that there is no liability of the public authority for injuries caused by a falling tree abutting a street or highway based on the rationale that any duty of the public authority with regard to the trees is a governmental duty. A public body, when exercising its governmental function, will only be liable if a statute permits liability. This concept is called governmental immunity.

A distinction exists with regard to acts of governmental agencies which are considered governmental functions and those which fall under the classification of proprietary functions. Proprietary functions are those which a municipality, in its discretion, may perform when considered to be for the best interests of the citizens of the municipality. Governmental functions are those activities which are carried on by a municipality pursuant to state requirement, in discharge of a state's obligation for health, safety or general welfare of the public generally, or which are voluntarily assumed by the municipality for the benefit of the general public rather than for its own citizens. The courts which have taken the view that municipalities will not be held liable for injuries caused by a falling tree abutting a street or highway, unless there is a statue in place which imposes a duty on a municipality to act, view the municipalities' function in this regard as a proprietary function.

For example, in *Dyer v. City of Danbury*,[78] an action was brought by the plaintiff against the city as a result of injuries sustained when the plaintiff was hit on the head by a falling limb from a dead tree which stood within the limits of the street. The street was a public highway of the city, and it was found that the tree had existed in a dangerous condition for more than a year. In deciding upon the issue of the city's liability in such a case, the Court in *Dyer* held that the duty of a city to remove a limb of a tree in a street overhanging a sidewalk and endangering travel as a result of its possibility to fall is a public governmental duty, for the neglect of which there is no duty unless imposed by statute.[79]

Does it make a difference if a municipality has enacted an ordinance requiring it to keep its streets and sidewalks in reasonable repair?

Even in the presence of an ordinance requiring a municipality to keep its highways, streets and sidewalks in reasonable repair, a municipality may still escape liability caused by the falling of a dead limb of a tree. In *Miller v. City of Detroit*,[80] the plaintiff brought an action against the city for injuries that resulted when the plaintiff was struck and injured by a dead limb which fell from a tree growing in the public street between the sidewalk and the curb. The city had in effect a statute which made it the duty of the city to keep streets, highways and sidewalks in reasonable repair and also to keep them reasonably safe for public travel.

The Court in *Miller* held that the statute was intended to require the maintenance of the physical surface of the state's highways in a reasonably safe condition against accidents from failure to do the things required by the statute, and not those due to extraneous causes. Obviously, the Court in *Miller* took a literal interpretation of the statute involved. The following section more aptly illustrates how the Courts handle cases dealing with injuries caused by municipal trees.

So who is responsible for trees which abut a street or highway?

In dealing with the issue with regard to trees growing along the street or highway, the courts must take into consideration issues involving the existence of government immunity as well as any statutes which provide for a duty by the city to maintain streets and highways in a reasonably safe condition.

One of the major areas of concern to residents of any municipality is the maintenance of street trees. Also the governing body of the municipality itself should be concerned with the maintenance of street trees which are either on city or private property. The foregoing sections have indicated that ordinarily a municipality will not be held liable for injuries caused by trees which abut a street or highway which are located on municipality property unless there is a duty imposed upon the municipality by statute for the maintenance of the trees. Furthermore, it was noted that even in the presence of a statute imposing a duty upon a municipality to maintain its trees, the municipality will only be liable if it fails to live up to a reasonable man standard commonly used in determining liability in negligence cases.

In order to understand how each of the foregoing concepts fit together, it seems appropriate to incorporate in its entirety an Ohio Attorney General Opinion issued in May of 1961, relative to the liability of municipal corporations to remove dangerous trees located both on private property and the public right-of-way.[81]

ATTORNEY GENERAL

2210

1. IT IS THE DUTY OF A BOARD OF TOWNSHIP TRUSTEES TO KEEP THE TOWNSHIP ROADS IN GOOD REPAIR: IT IS THEIR DUTY TO REMOVE AN OBSTRUCTING TREE EVEN IF PROPERTY OWNERS ALONG THE ROAD OWN UP TO THE CENTER OF THE ROAD.

2. WHERE A TREE LOCATED ON PRIVATE PROP- ERTY ALONG A TOWNSHIP ROAD HAS DANGEROUS BRANCHES HUNG OVER THE ROAD, REMOVAL IS THE DUTY PRIMARILY OF THE OWNER, BUT TOWNSHIP TRUSTEES ARE OBLIGATED TO RE- MOVE SAID TREE BY SUCH PROCEEDINGS AS NUISANCE ABATEMENT.

3. IT IS THE DUTY OF A MUNICIPAL CORPORA- TION TO REMOVE A DEAD TREE LOCATED IN A STREET RIGHT-OF-WAY IN SAID CORPORATION COSTS MAY BE ASSESSED AGAINST THE OWNER OF THE ABUTTING PROPERTY.

4. IT IS THE DUTY OF THE OWNERS OF A PIECE OF PRIVATE PROPERTY IN A MUNICIPAL CORPO- RATION TO REMOVE OVERHANGINGS FROM HIS PROPERTY OVER A PUBLIC STREET—THE MUNICI- PAL CORPORATION ALSO IS RESPONSIBLE TO PRO- TECT THE USERS OF THE STREET AND MAY INSTI- TUTE ABATEMENT PROCEEDINGS—Sections 5571.02, R.C. 3767.03, R.C. 927.02, R.C. 727.01, R.C. 3767.03, R.C. 927.22, R.C.

Syllabus:

1. Pursuant to the provisions of Section 5571.02, Revised Code, it is the duty of a board of township trustees to keep the township roads in good repair; and where a dead tree in a dangerous condition is located within the road right-of-way, the board has a duty to remove the tree even though property owners along the road own to the center of the road.

2. Where a tree is located on private property along a township road, but dead branches of the tree overhang the road and are dangerous to travelers on the road, the property owner has the primary duty

to remove the dangerous condition, although the board of township trustees is also obligated to remove said dangerous condition; and the board may institute nuisance abatement proceedings under Section 3767.03, Revised Code, to compel the property owner to remove the danger, or the board may request that the director of agriculture act pursuant to Section 927.22, Revised Code, to alleviate the dangerous condition.

3. Where a dead tree is located in a street right-of-way in a municipal corporation and the tree is in a condition causing danger to users of the street, it is the duty of the municipal corporation to remove the tree; and pursuant to Section 727.01, Revised Code, the municipal corporation may assess the costs of removal of the tree against the abutting property owner.

4. Where in a municipal corporation a dead tree is located on private property but overhangs a public street so as to cause danger to users of the street, the owner of the property has the primary duty to remove the dangerous condition but the municipal corporation also has a responsibility to protect users of the street; and the municipal corporation may institute nuisance abatement proceedings under Section 3767.03, Revised Code, to compel the property owner to remove the dangerous condition, or may request that the director of agriculture act pursuant to Section 927.22, Revised Code, to alleviate the dangerous condition.

Columbus, Ohio, May 25, 1961

Hon. George E. Schroeder, Prosecuting Attorney
Putnam County, Ottawa, Ohio

Dear Sir:

Your request for my opinion reads as follows:

"The Dutch Elm disease is causing a considerable tree removal problem, and several of the political subdivisions in my County have asked questions on which I would like to have your opinion. The questions are as follows:

"1. In a township where the property owners own to the center of the road, and a dead tree in a dangerous condition is located between the edge of the pavement and the edge of the road right of way, is it the obligation of the township trustees or the adjoining land owner to remove said tree, and if it is the obligation of the property owner, what can be done to compel its removal?

"2. In a township where the property owners own to the center of the road, and a tree is located on the adjoining owner's land outside the right of way, but has large dead limbs overhanging the highway endangering the users of said highway, is it the obligation of the trustees or the land owner to remove said tree, and if it is the obligation of the land owner, and he refuses to remove said tree, what can be done to compel this removal?

"3. In a municipal corporation, where there is no ordinance covering trees, and a dead tree is located between the sidewalk and curb within the street right of way, and said tree is in a dangerous condition, is it the responsibility of the village or the adjoining land owner to remove said tree, and if it is the responsibility of the adjoining property owner, what can be done to compel its removal?

"4. In a municipal corporation, where there is no ordinance covering trees, and a dead tree is located on private property, but overhanging a public street or alley in a dangerous condition, is it the responsibility of the village or property owner to remove said tree, and if it is the responsibility of the property owner, and he fails to remove said tree, what can be done to compel its removal?

"I have read the sections of the Code in regard to this problem, but have not found complete satisfaction. All these political subdivisions whom I represent are, of course, interested in knowing the situations in which it would be the responsibility of the property owner and if so, how, upon their refusal, to compel them to remove the tree or compel them to pay for the removal of the tree. I believe this problem is of interest to many political subdivisions in the State of Ohio due to the prevalence of Dutch Elm disease and an opinion from you, completely covering this whole field, would be greatly appreciated. I believe, by all of us."

Considering your first question, Section 5571.02, Revised Code, reads in part as follows:

"The board of township trustees shall have control of the township roads of its township and shall keep them in good repair. . . .

Thus, it is the positive duty of a board of township trustees to maintain and keep in good repair the township roads under its control; and it would appear that the presence on a road, or the road right-of-way, of trees which are dangerous to travel over the road, would require that the board take action to remove the trees, though not expressly granted by statute, arises by necessary implication from the statutory direction to keep the township roads in good repair.

In the particular situation as set out in the first question, in which the tree is in the road right-of-way, the township is in control of the roadway. Although the fee is in another, the use is, by nature of an easement, in the public and the landowner cannot freely use the property as he may desire. Since this land is really in the control of the public (it is "in the charge" of the board of township trustees as required under Section 927.22 infra.) it would be the responsibility of the board of township trustees to remove this dead or diseased tree and not the responsibility of the abutting property owner.

I note that Section 5543.14, Revised Code, also deals with the control of trees in a township road. This section reads:

"With the consent of the abutting landowner the county engineer shall have control of all trees and shrubs in the county roads of his county and the board of township trustees shall have control of all trees and shrubs in the township roads of its township. The department of agriculture or other proper department may, with the consent of the proper authorities and abutting landowner, take charge of the care of such trees. Such department may, with the consent of the proper authorities of the township, county, or state, plant trees along the public highway and may use any funds available for the development of forestry in the state to pay the expense of the planting and care of such trees. The ownership of all trees, so planted, shall remain in the public.''

(Emphasis added)

While this statute might be interpreted to limit the board's control over the trees and shrubs in the township roads to cases where consent of the abutting landowner has been obtained, the statute evidently refers to trees and shrubs which are not dead or diseased and which do not interfere with travel on the road, and does not pertain to diseased trees constituting a danger to travel on the road. Thus, I do not believe that the statute should be interpreted to affect my conclusion as to the first question.

In your second situation in which the dead tree is wholly outside of the right-of-way, but has large dead limbs overhanging the highway, and endangering the users of such highway, it would appear to be the obligation of the abutting property owner to trim his tree and, if necessary, destroy and remove the tree itself. In addition to such obligation of the property owner, the board would, of course, be authorized to remove limbs overhanging the road and endangering travel on the road; but I would assume that removal by the board in this set of circumstances would be done only in case of emergency.

Regarding the method to pursue to compel a property owner to remove a dangerous tree, it would appear that the tree would constitute a nuisance within the purview of Chapter 3767, Revised Code, and that the board would be authorized to initiate proceedings under Section 3767.03, Revised Code, to abate the nuisance. Also, the state director of agriculture has certain powers under Section 927.22, Revised Code, to eliminate infested or diseased trees and the board of township trustees could request that the department take action in a particular instance. Said Section 927.22 reads as follows:

''If the inspector or deputy finds on examination any nursery, greenhouse, field or farm, crop, orchard, small fruit plantation, park, cemetery, or any private or public premises, infested or infected with injurious insects or plant disease, he shall notify the owner or person having charge of such premises to that effect, and the owner or person having charge of the premises shall within seven days after such notice cause the removal and destruction of such trees, plants, shrubs, or other plant material, if they cannot be successfully treated; otherwise such owner or person shall cause them to be treated or apply any other preventive or remedial measures for the control or retardment of said injurious insects or plant disease on said premises as the director of agriculture may direct. Preventive measures shall be required and shall be enforced in the same manner on any such additional premises in the vicinity of the premises where said injurious insect or plant disease was found as seems necessary in accordance with the judgment of the director. No damages shall be awarded to the owner for the loss or destruction of infested or infected trees, plants, shrubs, or other plant material, or reimbursement made for expenses incurred incident to the application of said prescribed preventive or remedial measures. Such infested or infected trees, plants, shrubs, or other plant material are a public nuisance.

"In case the owner or person in charge of such premises refuses or neglects to carry out the orders of the director within seven days after receiving written notice, the director may proceed to treat or destroy the infested or infected plants or plant material or to apply any other necessary preventive or remedial measure. The expense shall be assessed, collected, and enforced, as taxes are assessed, collected, and enforced, against the premises upon which such expense was incurred. The amount of such expense when collected shall be paid to the director and by him deposited with the treasurer of state."

Coming to your third question which regards the situation where a dead tree is on the tree lawn in a village, Section 723.01, Revised Code, reads as follows:

"Municipal corporations shall have special power to regulate the use of the streets. The legislative authority of such municipal corporation shall have the care, supervision, and control of public highways, streets, avenues, alleys, sidewalks, public grounds, bridges, aqueducts and viaducts within the municipal corporation, and shall cause them to be kept open, in repair, and free from nuisance.''

As to a tree lawn, it is generally acceptable that the same is included as a part of the highway. The case of *Hubler v. Dayton*, 26 Ohio Law Abs., 679. at page 681, cites the statement in the case of *Barnesville v. Ward*, 85 Ohio St., 1, that the ''court recognized that the strip between the sidewalk and curb, ordinarily spoken of as the treelawn is a part of the highway and, therefore, the municipality is under the statutory obligation to keep it open, in repair and free from nuisance, as against the usual mode of travel.''

It will further be noted that Section 727.01, Revised Code, grants to municipal corporations the power to levy and collect special assessments on abutting property owners for costs connected with removing shade trees from a public road. Thus, although the municipal corporation has the responsibility of removing a dangerous tree from a tree lawn, the abutting owner may be assessed for the costs of removal.

Specifically answering your third question, I conclude that the municipal corporation and not the adjoining landowner would be responsible for the removal of a diseased tree located between the sidewalk and curb within the street right-of-way in a municipal corporation.

As to your fourth question regarding a dead tree on private property, but with limbs overhanging the public street, the owner of the tree would appear to be primarily responsible for removing the danger to people using the street. The municipal corporation does, however, also have a duty in this regard. As stated in the case of *Yackee, Adm., v. Napoleon*, 135 Ohio St., 344, at page 349:

''A municipal corporation holds the fee in its streets in trust for the purpose of public travel and transportation, subject to the right of the state to direct the method and manner by which such trust shall be administered and is charged at all times by reason of Section 3714, General Code, with the inescapable duty to keep such streets open, in repair and free from nuisance. This duty and requirement extends to the space above as well to the surface of the street. 'The public right goes to the full width of the street and extends indefinitely upward and downward so far at least as to prohibit encroachment upon such limits by any person by any means by which the enjoyment of such public right is or may be in any manner hindered or obstructed or made inconvenient or dangerous.' 44. Corpus Juris, 1007, note. . . . 'There is no sound reason why the duty of a municipal corporation to keep its streets "in safe condition" should not require it to take reasonable precautions against dangers from overhead as well as under foot.' " *Bohen v. City of Waseca*, 32 Minn., 176; 19 N.W., 730, 50 Am. Rep., 564. See also *Hume v. Mayor*, 74 N.Y., 264."

And at page 350 of the same case:

". . . This is a responsibility from which the municipality cannot relieve itself by any attempt to place the performance of such duty upon another. . . .

"If the municipality fails in this duty, and its failure results in injury to one lawfully using such street, it becomes liable to him in an action at law for damages. . . . and, even where the nuisance or dangerous condition in its street is created by another without its authority a municipality is nevertheless liable to one receiving an injury because of such nuisance, if the injury occurs after it acquires actual knowledge of the existence of such nuisance, or after sufficient time has elapsed that under the circumstances it should have acquired knowledge of the existence thereof."

The case of *Taylor v. Cincinnati*, 143 Ohio St., 426, dealt with a city's liability for absolute nuisances or qualified nuisances situated in the area of the street. The fifth paragraph of the syllabus of that case reads:

"The duty resting upon municipal corporations, under Section 3714, General Code, to keep their streets and other public ways open, in repair and free from nuisance, requires only reasonable care and vigilance, in view of all the surroundings, to keep such street and ways in a reasonably safe condition for travel in the usual and ordinary modes, and does not exact that which is unreasonable or impracticable. Municipal corporations are not insurers of the safety of their public ways, and are liable only for negligence in creating a faulty condition in such ways, or in failing to repair, remove or guard against defects or obstructions therein, after actual or constructive notice of their existence. The standard of care required to be exercised by municipal authorities in keeping streets in repair and free from nuisance is that care which persons of reasonable and ordinary prudence exercise under like circumstances and conditions.''

To answer your fourth question, therefore, I am of the opinion that the primary duty of removing a dead or diseased tree located on private property, but creating a danger to people using the adjoining street, is on the owner of the property, but that since the municipal corporation might be held liable for injuries incurred by persons using the street, the municipal corporation should take all necessary steps to remove the dangers. As with the board of township trustees discussed in the second question, the municipal corporation could initiate proceedings for the abatement of the nuisance under Section 3767.03, supra, or could request that the state director of agriculture proceed under Section 927.22, supra.

Since your letter of request specifically mentions elm disease, I believe I should make some mention of Sections 927.39 to 927.42, inclusive, Revised Code, which sections deal specifically with the combating of elm disease and phloem necrosis. These sections grant counties, townships and municipal corporations the authority to purchase equipment to combat elm disease and to hire employees to operate this equipment. Authority is also given these political subdivisions to authorize an agent to inspect lands within the subdivision with the permisstion of the landowner. Agents may enter onto private land to spray and treat trees, or to destroy and remove such, at the cost of the landowner. The Department of Agriculture of Ohio or that of the United States may be called for assistance. The statement in the statute that the cost will be assessed to the landowner would indicate that, although the subdivision may take it upon itself to eliminate the diseased or infected trees, the landowner is still the responsible party and the statute is not intended to shift such resposibility.

In summary, therefore, it is my opinion and you are advised:

1. Pursuant to the provisions of Section 5571.02, Revised Code, it is the duty of a board of township trustees to keep the township roads in good repair: and where a dead tree in a dangerous condition is located within the road right-of-way, the board has a duty to remove the tree even though property owners along the road own to the center of the road.

2. Where a tree is located on private property along a township road, but dead branches of the tree overhang the road and are dangerous to travelers on the road, the property owner has the primary duty to remove the dangerous condition, although the board of township trustees is also obligated to remove said dangerous condition: and the board may institute nuisance abatement proceedings under Section 3767.03, Revised Code, to compel the property owner to remove the danger, or the board may request that the director of agriculture act pursuant to Section 927.22, Revised Code, to alleviate the dangerous condition.

3. Where a dead tree is located in a street right-of-way in a municipal corporation and the tree is in a condition causing danger to users of the street, it is the duty of the municipal corporation to remove the tree: and pursuant to Section 727.01, Revised Code, the municipal corporation may assess the costs of removal of the tree against the abutting property owner.

4. Where in a municipal corporation a dead tree is located on private property but overhangs a public street so as to cause danger to users of the street, the owner of the property has the primary duty to remove the dangerous condition but the municipal corporation also has a responsibility to protect users of the street: and the municipal corporation may institute nuisance abatement proceedings under Section 3767.03, Revised Code, to compel the property owner to remove the dangerous condition, or may

request that the director of agriculture act pursuant to Section 927.22, Revised Code, to alleviate the dangerous condition.

Respectfully,
Mark McElroy
Attorney General

As can be seen in reviewing Ohio Attorney General Opinion 2210, a municipality is liable for injuries caused by trees located on public property which obstruct the streets or highways. Furthermore, although the property owner is primarily responsible for eliminating a dead tree or one which is defective and which is located on private property but which is adjacent to the public street, municipalities can also be held responsible for injuries caused by the hazardous trees due to the Ohio statute which requires the municipality to protect the users of its streets.

The best advice for the municipality is to be on the look-out for all hazardous trees, whether located on public or private property, adjacent to the street or highway. As previously noted, in either case the reasonable man standard is used to determine whether the municipality was negligent in failing to act.

What liability does a municipality have with regard to trees located on public grounds which do not abut a street or highway?

Liability in this instance is governed by the same duties and standard of care imposed upon private landowners. Public grounds consist of recreational land and nonrecreational land. Liability of the municipality in relation to recreational land has been previously discussed under the topic of recreational user statutes. Liability of the municipality for injuries caused on public grounds is premised on the municipality's duty to keep its public grounds in repair and free from nuisance.

Liability of the municipality generally arises out of a statute which waives immunity for injuries caused by a municipality's failure to keep its public grounds free from nuisance. Ohio has such a statute. Ohio Revised Code Section 2744.02(3) states:

> (3) Political subdivisions are liable for injury, death, or loss to persons or property caused by their failure to keep roads, highways, streets, avenues, alleys, sidewalks, bridges, aqueducts, viaducts, or public grounds within the political subdivisions open, in repair, and free from nuisance, except that it is a full defense to such liability, when a bridge within a municipality corporation is involved, that municipal corporation does not have the responsibility for maintaining or inspecting the bridges.

With regard to municipal trees growing on public grounds, the municipality will be held liable for injuries caused by a tree under common law principals of negligence if there is a statute present which waives governmental immunity. The best advice to any municipality is to take precautions to keep trees growing on municipal grounds free from hazard regardless of any governmental immunity statutes which might be in effect.

Are individuals held to a different standard of care than municipalities for injuries caused by trees abutting streets or highways?

No, the reasonable man standard is also used in determining liability of an individual property owner who has a tree on such property abutting a city street or highway which causes injury. This situation usually arises when a passing individual is hit by a falling tree, which is defective due to age.

Is there a distinction in terms of a duty of care between an urban and rural landowner?

Yes, when applying the reasonable man standard, the courts have made a distinction between the urban and the rural landowner. For example, in *Heckert v. Patrick*,[82] a negligence action was brought against a property owner and the county board of commissioners for personal injuries and property damage sustained when a tree limb fell upon a rural highway into the immediate path of the plaintiff's motorcycle.

In deciding upon the issues of liability in *Heckert*, the Court held that generally an owner of land abutting a highway may be held liable on negligence principles for injuries resulting from a tree or limb falling onto the highway. It was recognized in *Heckert* that a distinction has developed throughout the United States which allows for a lesser standard of care with reference to rural land as opposed to strictly urban property.

What duty exists for the urban landowner?

It is generally recognized that the urban landowner has a duty of reasonable care relative to the tree, including inspection to make sure that the tree is safe.[83] The justification for this distinction results from the fact that a rural landowner could have trees resembling a forest in dimension, thus a forced inspection standard would be unreasonable. In contrast, the urban landowner generally owns only a few trees which would not make the duty of inspection an unreasonable burden. It is important to note that the standards set forth by the *Heckert* Court are applicable to both the private owner of property and the public authority.[84]

What duty exists for the rural landowner?

A leading case dealing with the rural landowner's duty with regard to trees growing on his property is *Hay v. Norwalk Lodge No. 730, B.P.O.E.*[85] In *Hay,* plaintiff's decedent was killed as a result of injuries when a defective tree growing upon the premises owned by the defendant fell on the cab of the decedent's truck while the decedent was traveling on a rural highway. In determining whether the owner of a premises abutting a rural highway is liable for injury caused by the falling of a defective tree, the Court held that, while there is no duty imposed upon the owner of property abutting a rural highway to inspect growing trees abutting that highway or to ascertain defects which may result in injury to a traveler on the highway, an owner having knowledge, actual or constructive, of a patently defective condition of a tree which may result in injury to a traveler must exercise reasonable care to prevent harm to a person using the highway from the falling of such a tree or its branches.[86]

The reason the courts seem to protect both the municipality and the landowner from liability is because trees are natural structures, and, as previously discussed, a landowner has no duty to protect others from natural structures. The cases cited make it quite clear that an urban landowner will be held to a slightly higher standard of forced constructive notice and knowledge with regard to trees growing adjacent to a street or highway. To the contrary, a rural landowner will be held liable if the landowner has actual or constructive knowledge that a tree growing adjacent to a street or highway is defective, however, constructive knowledge does not include knowledge the rural landowner would have obtained if such landowner inspected the tree. The reason for this distinction is that a rural landowner has no duty to inspect the trees on such property.

Chapter 6

Governmental Liability for Failure to Maintain Vegetation Around Intersections and Railroad Crossings

An issue of law with regard to trees which appears to be drawing greater attention involves governmental liability for a municipality's failure to properly maintain trees which obscure view at railroad crossings or at street or highway intersections. The dangers brought about by such failures of municipalities to properly maintain trees in this regard have given rise to successful suits by injured parties against municipalities for injuries sustained as a result of the municipalities' failure to perform their duties and obligations.

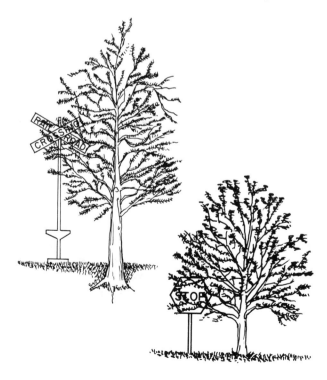

Are governmental agencies generally liable for damages caused by their failure to maintain vegetation around intersections and railroad crossings?

Yes, the courts are generally holding municipalities liable for damages caused by their failure to maintain vegetation around intersections and railroad crossings.[87]

Under what circumstances is a municipality generally found liable for damages?

The cases which allow liability on the part of the government generally involve states which have statutes and ordinances which prescribe a municipality's responsibilities regarding vegetation growing on public property. However, there are states in which courts have held municipalities liable strictly on principles of negligence.

What is the underlying rationale for finding that no liability exists?

There are states which do not find liability on the part of municipalities for their failure to maintain trees around intersections and railroad crossings and such states generally base their opinions on the grounds that a municipality has no duty to reduce vegetation obscuring an intersection view and that the growth of vegetation beside the street itself does not constitute a defect in the road.[88]

Do courts ever take into consideration the negligence of the individual who was injured to determine whether liability exists?

Yes, there are courts which take into consideration whether the person who was injured was contributorily negligent or whether the accident was caused by another driver's negligence in making their determination as to a municipality's liability for failing to maintain or remove vegetation.[89]

A case involving a statute which holds a municipality liable for injuries arising out of its failure to reduce vegetation obscuring a motorists' view is *Bentley v. Saunemin Township*.[90] In this particular case, a lawsuit was brought arising out of an automobile collision at the intersection of a township road and a state highway caused by the overhanging branches of a tree obstructing the vision of a stop sign on the road. The Court in *Bentley* allowed a verdict against both the township and the highway commissioner observing that a state statute made the maintenance of township roads a responsibility of its highway commissioner. The Court further held that (1) the township and its highway commissioner owed the motorist a duty of reasonable care in maintaining visibility of the stop sign; (2) and that the township and its highway commissioner failed to perform this duty entitling the motorist to recover damages. An important point in this case is that even though the Court recognized the existence of a statute calling for a duty to remove vegetation by the township, the Court went even further to note that there was no evidence that the driver, by virtue of prior travel in the area, might have known of the presence of the intersection or stop sign.

The importance of this point was brought out in a recent case in the State of Illinois, *Norwell v. Fancy Creek Township*.[91] In *Norwell*, an action was brought against a township to recover for injuries sustained by a motorcyclist and his passenger in a motorcycle/automobile collision at an intersection of a state highway and township road wherein it was alleged that a stop sign was obscured by vegetation. The Court in ruling in favor of the township in that case found that the motorcyclist was so inattentive that he would not have seen the stop sign even had it not been obscured, that he was going too fast to stop and, instead, decided it was best to attempt to cross the intersection as fast as possible. This case is important in the respect that the Court did take into consideration the acts of the motorist in comparing them to the actions or inactions of the township in failing to properly maintain the intersection as required.[92]

Even though the township in that case was able to escape liability, the point to be made by that case with regard to any municipality is that time should be taken to properly maintain trees which grow at or near intersections and railroad crossings; it will help to promote safety, beautify the area and, of course, help to avoid needless and costly litigation.

Chapter 7

When Must a Public Utility Compensate a Landowner for the Destruction of Trees Growing on the Landowner's Property

An issue which the courts have been often faced with is when must a public utility compensate a landowner for the destruction of the landowner's trees. This situation usually involves the right or authority of a public utility to trim, cut or remove shade trees which abut the streets of a municipality for the maintenance of the utility company's service.

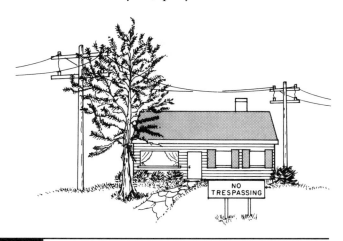

What right does a public utility have to cut or trim trees?

It is generally held that a public utility has no right to trim, cut or remove shade trees growing on the street of a municipality, unless there is some authority granted to the utility company by the municipality to do so. For example, in *Cartwright v. Liberty Telephone Co.*,[93] the plaintiffs brought suit against the defendant public utility company to recover damages for injuries caused to their property by the cutting of their ornamental and shade trees by the defendant utility company. It was proven that the defendant telephone company never had been granted a franchise to conduct a telephone business in the city.

In determining the issue of liability, the Court in *Cartwright* ruled that a telephone company not shown to have been granted a franchise to conduct a telephone business in the city, or authorized to use the city streets, could not defend against a cause of action for mutilating trees growing in a city street on the ground that the erection and maintenance of telephone lines is a proper use of a street, and that trees interfering with that use may be rightfully cut. It would appear that any authority that a public utility would have to trim or cut trees on a landowner's property must come from the authorization of the city and its right to remove or trim trees where they interfere with a proper use of the street.[94]

However, there seems to be a difference of judicial opinion concerning the rights and liabilities of a public utility with regard to the cutting or mutilating of shade trees for the purpose of stringing wires or erecting poles pursuant to authority granted by the public authority. There have been some courts which hold that public authorities have no right to permit public utilities to remove or mutilate trees without compensation to the landowner where the fee to the highway is owned by the landowner. For example, in *Daily v. State*,[95] an action was brought by the plaintiff for the destruction of certain shade trees by the defendant. The Court in *Daily* recognized that an owner of land adjoining a public highway, whose title extends to the center of the road and who has cultivated shade trees planted partly on his own land and partly in the line of the highway has a property interest in the trees.[96] The Court also held that while a legislature may authorize the construction of a telegraph line by a telegraph company upon a public highway, this authority does not empower the company to injure the property of an adjoining landowner, nor to appropriate any of the landowner's property rights in the highway unless compensation is first made. On the other hand, it has been held that if the trees were on a fee owned by a municipality as in urban areas, then the destruction was not compensable.

What test is used to determine whether a utility company's actions in cutting or trimming a tree are proper?

At least in Ohio, the test for the determination of compensation for the destruction of trees has changed. The distinction between rural and urban, and who owned the fee has been eliminated. For example, in *Ziegler v. Ohio Water Service Co.*,[97] a landowner brought suit for an injunction to prevent a water company from entering upon the landowner's premises until an easement had been negotiated.

In determining what compensation was owing to the landowner for the intrusion by the utility company, the Court ruled that the construction and maintenance of an underground water pipeline for public purposes in real property subject to an easement for highway purposes was not an added burden on the property for which compensation must be awarded. In accordance with *Ziegler*, the test for the determination of compensation for the destruction of trees became whether the intended use of the land, subject to the easement of the state for a highway, is an added burden on the landowner's property.[98]

The test set out in *Ziegler* was also followed in the case of *Ohio Edison Co. v Carroll*.[99] In *Carroll*, the electric utility brought an action against the property owner to obtain an easement on the owner's property to install wires for communication between electric substations. The Court in *Carroll* found that the wires to be installed were necessary for the operation and maintenance of an electric plant.[100] The Court also concluded that an electric company's use of the country roadway to maintain its poles and wires was not an additional burden upon the fee of the abutting property owner for which the owner was entitled to compensation. Based on this test, the court will look to see if the intrusion to the property owner's land is unreasonable in order to determine whether compensation to the landowner should be allowed.[101]

Other jurisdictions appear to follow the "necessary and reasonableness" test used in Ohio in determining whether compensation for the destruction or trimming of trees by a public utility is owing to a property owner. For example, in *Johnson v. City of Chattanooga*,[102] an action was brought by a landowner against the City of Chattanooga to recover for damages resulting from the trimming of a shade tree. The City of Chattanooga owned and operated a public service system for the lighting of its streets and the private homes and other buildings of the city. Incident to this operation, it erected poles and strung wires along its streets, and when necessary cut and trimmed trees along the street for the maintenance of those poles and wires. In effect, the City of Chattanooga operated as a public utility.

In deciding upon the issue of what compensation was owed by the City of Chattanooga for the trimming of the landowner's tree, the Court held that the use of the street for poles and wires required for the lighting of the street by electricity was within a reasonable range of its right to use streets derived from an easement for street purposes. The Court in *Johnson* held that no additional burden was imposed upon the plaintiff for which he was entitled to compensation as the trimming of the plaintiff's tree was necessary for the stringing and maintenance of the electric wire.[103]

What steps should be followed to determine if liability exists on the part of a utility for the cutting down or trimming of a landowner's tree?

Taking into consideration the aforementioned cases as a whole, it would appear that certain steps must be followed to determine whether liability exists on the part of a utility company for the cutting or trimming of a landowner's tree. The first step is to determine whether the utility company even had the authority to trim or remove such trees. If such authority was present, the next determination to be made is whether or not an easement is present on the property owner's premises which would allow the public utility to enter upon the owner's land. After finding that such an easement does, in fact, exist, the courts will then look to see if the intended use of the land by the utility company, subject to the easement, is an added burden on the property owner's land. In making this determination, the courts will look to see if the proposed intrusion is unreasonable. It seems clear that when the authority exists allowing a public utility company to remove or trim trees which are necessary for the maintenance and installation of its facilities, that a land owner will not be able to recover damages to the landowner's trees so long as there is no unnecessary damage done to the landowner's property.

What is the underlying rationale for a utility company's right to trim and cut trees growing on a landowner's property?

The authority on this subject makes it clear that a landowner's property interest in trees is subservient to a public utility company's right to remove and trim trees which interfere with the necessary and reasonable operations of the public utility company. The right of the general public to receive the benefits public utilities provide supercedes the rights of a property owner to have trees located on the landowner's property untouched.

Will a public utility escape liability if it hires an independent contractor to cut or trim trees in the maintenance of its lines?

An interesting situation sometimes occurs when a public utility tries to avoid liability for the cutting of trees on a landowner's property by hiring an independent contractor to do the work. For example, in *National Rating Bureau v. Florida Power Corporation*,[104] an action was brought by an abutting land owner to enjoin an electric utility from occupying a one hundred foot strip without payment and for damages for cutting certain trees. It would appear that the utility company had contracted with an independent contractor for the cutting of trees along the right-of-way and that the independent contractor had inadvertently cut trees on adjoining property. It is important to note that the public utility did not have the right to cut down the trees along the street in this case without compensating the landowner for such trees. Since the public utility would have itself been liable to the landowner for the destruction of the landowner's trees, the Court ruled that the utility company was liable to the landowner for damages occasioned by the cutting, despite the independent contractor status of the person who did the actual cutting.[105]

What rights do public utility companies possess with regard to the removal of obstructions located within the easement.

It is generally recognized that where a property owner unlawfully obstructs or interferes with the easement of an easement holder, the holder of the easement has the authority to remove those obstructions. In the case of *Rueckel v. Texas Eastern Transmission Corporation*,[106] the plaintiffs brought a lawsuit against the defendant utility company seeking damages for pine trees which were damaged or destroyed in the course of maintenance operations carried out by the public utility company within the easement area. The plaintiff landowners further sought a determination by the Court as to whether the defendant utility company must compensate the plaintiff for the removal of the trees and whether the plaintiffs had the future right to plant trees within the easement.

The Court in *Rueckel* held that the landowners were not entitled to grow trees on the utility company's right-of-way that either obstructed, unreasonably burdened, or interfered with the exercise of the easement rights and that the utility company had the right to remove the trees without compensating the landowners. The Court in *Rueckel* further held that the proper test for determining whether the landowners were entitled to damages from the utility company for the removal of the landowner's trees located within the easement holder's right-of-way was to determine whether the existence of the object for which compensation was claimed, the right to grow trees, represented an exercise by the property owner of a retained property right or an infringement upon the easement holder's rights.

What activities are public utilities entitled to engage in without the presence of an easement?

Generally, the view is taken that a public utility has no legal right to cut, trim or remove trees growing on the property of a private landowner without the presence of an express easement in favor of the utility company over the land. Furthermore, a public utility has no legal right to cut, trim or remove trees growing on public streets without the express permission from the public authority. It is generally recognized that only if a tree is located on private property which is encroaching onto or over public land does the public authority have the legal power to grant a utility company permission to trim the tree. Under those circumstances, the tree must be interfering with a proper use of the street or public right-of-way.

However, when the covenants on the land-owner's deed specify that the ownership to the street is owned by the landowner, it is a private street. Under those circumstances, it is generally recognized that the public authority has no right to permit utility companies to remove or trim trees without first providing compensation to the landowner. If the trees are on city-owned land, then the city may empower utility companies to remove, cut or trim trees without compensating the adjacent landowner. In this instance, the trimming or removal must actually be required, and must be performed in a reasonable manner. If the trimming is done in a negligent fashion, then either the landowner or the public authority may be able to recover damages against the utility company.[107]

Chapter 8

Is a Property Owner Entitled to Compensation When the Owner's Trees are Injured or Destroyed Due to the Application of Herbicides and Pesticides by Another?

Yes. Injuries caused to a property owner's trees as a result of the negligent application of herbicides and pesticides by another are compensable. This area of the law seems to be drawing greater attention as the trend toward environmental consciousness grows. Liability for the negligent application of herbicides and pesticides is based both on common law principles of negligence and by statute—both of which will be discussed in the following sections.

What are some typical examples of herbicide damage?

An excellent case dealing with herbicide damage is *Marion J. Gilbreath v. Veldkamp's Flowers, Inc.*[108] The property owner, Marion J. Gilbreath, brought suit against Veldkamp's Flowers, Inc. claiming that his property was damaged as a result of a weed killer which leaked onto Mr. Gilbreath's property, destroying his trees and shrubs. Veldkamp's owned a greenhouse adjacent to Mr. Gilbreath's property and it was alleged that employees of Veldkamp's used a herbicide known as Pramitol, which drained out of the greenhouse and onto Mr. Gilbreath's property causing damages to his trees and shrubs. Mr. Gilbreath was awarded damages in the amount of $375,000.00 resulting from Veldkamp's negligent application of the soil sterilant.[109]

The case of *Steven S. Roberts et. al. v. Colorado Weed Control et. al.*,[110] is another excellent

69

illustration of a herbicide damages case. Mr. and Mrs. Roberts contracted with Colorado Weed Control to eradicate weeds in special areas of the Roberts' property. The Roberts sought assurances from Colorado Weed for the protection of certain trees located on the Roberts' property which were located near the areas to be sprayed by Colorado Weed. The Roberts were assured that the weed killing process would be safe and would not threaten the trees in question.

In August of 1979, Colorado Weed applied the product known as Hyvar-X to the specified areas of the Roberts' property. The active ingredient in Hyvar-X is Bromacil, which is a soil sterilant which acts by preventing vegetation from obtaining nourishment from the soil, thereby causing the plant to wither and die. Although the spraying by Colorado Weed was successful in eliminating the undesired weeds, the Roberts began to notice that the leaves of their Gamble Oak trees located near the areas sprayed were turning brown.[111]

The Roberts informed Colorado Weed of the problem. Colorado Weed advised the Roberts that heavy watering of the affected areas might help and might wash away the chemicals. Acting on Colorado Weed's advice, the Roberts watered all the areas heavily. By the fall of 1979, all affected trees, shrubs and vegetation were dead, including hundreds of Gamble Oak trees up to 100 years old.[112]

The Roberts brought a lawsuit against Colorado Weed and expert testimony was presented that Bromacil was the cause of the soil contamination and vegetation damages in the specified areas of the Roberts' property. The Court in the *Roberts* case found that the Roberts' trees were killed by Bromacil. The Court further held that the proximate cause of the extensive damages and killing of the desirable plant life was the intensive watering of the affected areas by the Roberts at the direction of Colorado Weed.[113]

The Court in *Roberts* found gross negligence to exist on the part of Colorado Weed due to Colorado Weed's superior knowledge of the chemical and through its failure to properly assess the damages and take proper remedial steps to curtail further damage. The Court awarded the Roberts exemplary damages due to Colorado Weed's lack of diligence and failure to take remedial steps, together with the highly improper and destructive advice by Colorado Weed to heavily water, which indicated a lack of recognition and concern for the damages presented by the herbicide as well as a lack of knowledge of the chemical used. The Court held that Colorado Weed's acts constituted reckless disregard of the rights and feelings of the Roberts'.[114]

Two points can be drawn from the *Roberts* case. The first point is that the applicator of the herbicide better be aware of the chemical make-up of the herbicide to be applied as well as the affects these chemicals may have on surrounding vegetation to the area the herbicide is to be applied. The second point to be made is that liability will be greater if the applicator of the herbicide engages in the negligent application of the herbicide and then fails to take measures to correct the damages which result or the applicator compounds the negligence by negligent corrective action. The applicator should be knowledgeable of the herbicide to be used and the affects the herbicide has on vegetation in the surrounding area in which it is to be applied.

What standard of care must be utilized in the application of herbicides and pesticides?

The case of *Alvin A. Sellon et. al. v. Thornton Flying Service*,[115] not only provides another excellent illustration involving the application of herbicides but it also sets forth the standard of care to be used in the application of herbicides. In the *Sellon* case, the Defendant, Thornton

Flying Service, was employed by an individual to spray two 80 acre strips of wheat on property which bordered the Sellons' property. The north side of the Sellons' property was protected by approximately 114 Siberian Elm trees.

The evidence in *Sellon* established that Thornton Flying Service used two different herbicides, both of which had label precautions warning the applicator that the products were capable of injuring broad leaf plants and trees and other desirable trees and plants. One of the herbicide labels warned the applicator to take certain steps to avoid chemical wind drift which included the warning that spraying should not take place when winds exceeded six to seven miles per hour. The other label suggested against aerial application when sensitive crops and plants were in the vicinity of the area to be treated.[116]

Thornton Flying Service made an aerial application of the herbicides in question on July 3, 1982. The evidence further revealed that an individual who was living on the Sellons' property witnessed chemical mist clouds head toward the Sellons' property and actually felt the chemical mist on his face. Expert testimony in the *Sellon* case revealed that the death or damage of the trees on the Sellons' property was due to the application of the herbicides.

The Court in the *Sellon* case held that Thornton Flying Service was negligent in spraying in an area where plants were susceptible to being damaged or destroyed by the types of herbicides being used. The Court further held that Thornton Flying Service failed to act with reasonable care under the circumstances to protect others from property damage.[117]

The *Sellon* case makes it clear that the standard to be used in the application of herbicides is reasonable care or the reasonable man standard which is applied in negligence cases.

Are there statutes governing the application of herbicides and pesticides?

Yes. The Court in the *Sellon* case referred to a statute entitled C.R.S. 35-10-111 which creates liability when a herbicide is applied in careless or negligent manner creating a hazard to adjacent property. The Court in *Sellon* made the indication that C.R.S. 35-10-111 was designed to protect against the type of injury inflicted upon the Sellons' property. The Court further noted that since the Sellons' property was located adjacent to the area sprayed by Thornton Flying Service, that the Sellons fell within the class to be protected by the statute. The Court noted that under such circumstances Thornton Flying Service was negligent per se.[118] Negligence per se simply means that Thornton Flying Service's actions in spraying the herbicides in an area where the Sellons' trees were susceptible to being damaged were negligent without any argument or proof as to the particular surrounding circumstances because such actions were violations of C.R.S. 35-10-111.

Many states have statutes which regulate the use of herbicides and pesticides. These statutes may even provide for civil and criminal penalties for their violation by the applicator. One example can be found in Ohio.

Ohio Revised Code Section 921.25 states in part:

> It is unlawful for any person:
>
> (A) To apply, use, supervise such application or use, or recommend a pesticide for use inconsistent with its labeling or other restriction imposed by the director of agriculture;
>
> (B) Unless directly supervised by a certified applicator, to use, or supervise the use of, a restricted use pesticide without being licensed or certified to do so;
>
> (C) To refuse or fail to keep and maintain records required by the director in rules

promulgated pursuant to this Chapter, or to make reports when and as required by the director in rules promulgated pursuant to this Chapter;

(D) Falsely or fraudulently to represent the effect of pesticides or methods to be utilized;

(E) To apply known ineffective or improper materials;

(F) To operate in a negligent manner, which includes operation of faulty or unsafe equipment;

(G) To impersonate any federal, state, county, or city official;

(H) To make false or fraudulent records, invoices, or reports;

(I) To use or supervise the use of restricted pesticide on the property of another without having a certified applicator in direct supervision;

(J) To use fraud or misrepresentation in making application for a license or certificate or renewal of a license or certificate;

(K) To refuse, fail, or neglect to comply with any limitations or restrictions of a license issued pursuant to Sections 921.01 to 921.29 of the Revised Code or rules thereunder;

(L) To aid or abet a licensee or another person to violate Sections 921.01 to 921.29 of the Revised Code or rules thereunder;

(M) To make a false or misleading statement in an inspection concerning any infestation or pests or the use of pesticides;

(N) To refuse or fail to comply with Sections 921.01 to 921.29 of the Revised Code, the rules adopted thereunder, or with any lawful order of the director;

(O) To distribute restricted use pesticides to the ultimate use at any time without a pesticide dealer's license;

(P) To use any pesticide which is under experimental use permit contrary to the provisions of such permit;

(Q) Who is licensed as a custom applicator to engage in fraudulent business practice in the application of pesticides;

(R) To dispose of any pesticide product or container in such a manner as to have unreasonable adverse effects on the environment;

(S) To display any pesticide in any manner to produce unreasonable adverse effects on the environment, or to contaminate adjacent food, feed, or other products.

Ohio Revised Code Section 921.26 creates civil penalties for violation of R.C. Section 921.25. Ohio Revised Code Section 921.99 creates criminal penalties for violations of R.C. Section 921.25 and for a second offense of division (F) or (M) of R.C. Section 921.25 the applicator can even be charged with a felony.

The case of *The State of Ohio v. Allied Pest Control*,[119] provides an illustration of the application of O.R.C. Section 921.25. Allied Pest Control was charged with three separate violations of O.R.C. Section 921.25, including application of a pesticide in a manner inconsistent with its labeling, the negligent operation of faulty equipment and the making of false and misleading statements in relation to inspection of infestation. Testimony in *Allied* was offered that Allied had improperly applied the pesticide known as Termide in its treatment of a particular residence. Testimony was also offered to suggest that Allied had not done a thorough and complete job of inspecting and treating the premises. However, further evidence revealed that the owner of the residence had stopped payment on the check to Allied for the contract to perform the work in question, as a result Allied considered its contract with the homeowner cancelled and elected not to complete any further work on the premises.[120]

The Court in *Allied* recognized that Allied had applied the pesticide in a poor and seemingly unprofessional manner. However, in deciding upon whether Allied's actions were negligent for purposes of sustaining a criminal conviction under the statute, the Court stated in its syllabus:

> A conviction for a violation of R.C. 921.25 (prohibiting the negligent application of pesticides) is against the manifest weight of the evidence where the evidence shows that the pesticide was applied in a poor and seemingly unprofessional manner. A lack of quality work in not a "substantial lapse from due care" needed to establish criminal negligence.

As can be seen in the *Allied* case, the standard for negligence in the application or use of a pesticide is different for the purposes of a criminal case as opposed to a civil case. Negligence in a civil case is determined by the reasonable care or reasonable man standard. A person acts negligently for the purpose of a criminal case when, because of a substantial lapse from due care, the person fails to perceive or avoid a risk that his conduct may cause a certain result or maybe of a certain nature.[121]

A point to be made with regard to the standard of care for the professional who is applying herbicides or pesticides is that the professional will be held to a higher standard of care than the ordinary individual due to the professional's knowledge and experience in the application of herbicides and pesticides. The standard of care used will be the same standard of care utilized by the trade in the geographical vicinity involved. The standard of care will be that standard of care

exercised by the reasonably prudent professional in the local area involved under the
circumstances.

Plates

Chapter 8 discusses various issues concerning trees injured or destroyed due to the application of pesticides and herbicides. The following photos represent actual cases involving herbicide damage.

BROMACIL—applied on gravel mulch for weed control. Killed all trees in planting area.

BROMACIL—applied on gravel drive for weed control. Roots coming in contact killed Gambel Oak 50 feet from source of application.

Same property as above.

BROMACIL—applied to gravel drive. Killed all mature trees that root came in contact with.

BROMACIL—bought and applied by mistake. Owner thought he was buying UREA, a high nitrogen fertilizer. In two weeks, his property looked like this from an aerial view.

The same property as above. A ground view. All the soil had to be removed and replaced 12 inches deep.

PRAMITOL—applied on opposite side of fence by neighbor. Absorbed by root system of this Linden tree growing under the fence.

PRAMITOL—applied by neighbor on rock mulch for weed control. Killed all of his neighbor's Poplar trees.

PRAMITOL 25E—applied under asphalt as weed control. Trees are dying from root contact under the asphalt.

PRAMITOL 25E—
applied under asphalt
as weed control—the
spiral effect in the Blue
Spruce is typical of
how the sterilant is
taken up by the root
system and translocated
into the tree.

PRAMITOL 25E—
applied under asphalt
as weed control. Pine
trees dying from root
contact.

BROMACIL—applied
before asphalt seal coat
as weed control in
cracks of old asphalt.
All close by trees dying
by root contact.

PRAMITOL 25E—
applied between con-
crete curb and gutter
and asphalt to help
eliminate weed growth.
Roots from Locusts tree
in lawn area growing
through expansion joint
cracks contacts sterilant
killing the tree.

TEBUTHIURON—
applied along county
road as weed control
was sufficient to kill all
the Elm trees around
this farmstead.

TEBUTHIURON-
TREFLURALIN—
mistakenly applied to
an open field for pre-
emergent and post-
emergent weed control
prior to planting seed-
ling nursery trees.

MAGNESIUM CHLORIDE—applied to county gravel road. The chemical is picked up in the root system of nearby trees.

2,4-DICHLORO-PHENOXY ACETETIC ACID—aerial application to croplands for weed control. Drift by excessive wind caused severe damage to adjoining trees.

2,4-DICHLORO-PHENOXY ACETIC ACID—aerial application to croplands for weed control. Drift by excessive wind caused severe damage to windbreak trees.

2,4-DICHLORO-PHENOXY ACETIC ACID—infrared photo of damage to windbreak trees around a farmstead caused by the drift. NOTE: The pale color on the outside row signifies the worst damage by the chemical.

3,6-DICHLORO-2-METHOXY BENZOIC ACID)—applied to lawn area as broad leaf weed control. Excessive use of this chemical caused the death of these Locust trees.

PHOTOS—Courtesy of Eugene B. Eyerly, a foremost investigator and appraiser of herbicide damages.

Chapter 9

Measure of Damages for Injury to or Destruction of Trees

What are the methods for determining damages for the destruction of trees?

A very important issue relating to trees involves the damages which are available for the destruction of or injury to the various types of trees growing on the landowner's property. Basically there are four major methods of determining damages for the destruction of trees on a landowner's property. These methods include: (1) the resulting depreciation in the value of the land on which the trees stood; (2) the cost of replacing destroyed or injured trees or restoring the premises on which they stood to their previous condition; (3) the value of the injured or destroyed trees themselves; and, (4) the resulting loss of aesthetic value or the resulting deprivation of the comfort and convenience which the trees provided the landowner. In order to gain an understanding of the theory behind each of these measures of damages, it is necessary to review the various fact patterns to which they have been applied.

Under what circumstances will the resulting depreciation in the value of the land be used to measure damages?

A case which relied upon the resulting depreciation of the land on which the trees stood as a measure of damages for their destruction is *Baillou v. Carl Bolander & Sons Co.*[122] In *Baillou*, an action was brought for the destruction of trees by a highway contractor. The Court in *Baillou* held that it has long been the rule that the measure of damages for the destruction of trees is the difference between the value of the land before and after the damage has been inflicted.[123] In deciding upon the measure of damages to be used, the Court placed reliance on the fact that the damaged trees had been unhealthy, deformed and crooked. The Court held that to adopt a replacement rule in the case would involve an expense greatly out of proportion to the actual damage to the real estate.[124]

In *Thatcher v. Lane Construction Co.*,[125] an action was brought for damages inflicted to the plaintiffs' lot by the defendants' removal of trees and underbrush. The Court in *Thatcher* held that the general rule which states that the measure of damages for injury to real estate shall not exceed the difference in market value before and immediately after the injury is not an arbitrary or exact formula to be applied in every case without regard to whether its application would compensate the injured party fully for losses sustained.[126] The Court further held that where the presence of trees was essential to the planned use of the property as a homesite in accordance with the taste and wishes of its owner, where not unreasonable, the owner could be awarded as damages the fair cost of restoring the owner's land to a reasonable approximation of its former condition.[127] In accordance with *Thatcher*, it would seem that the courts which hold that the proper measure of damages for the destruction of or injury to trees is the difference in the value of the land just before and just after the injury, such courts also recognize factors other than the contemplated use of the land in assessing the depreciation in the value of the land.

In *Cy Carney Appliance Company v. True*,[128] an action was brought for the destruction of a house and also for the destruction of shade trees on a farm as a result of fire. The Court in True held that the proper measure of damages for destruction of the trees was the difference between the market value of the farm of the plaintiffs' before and after the destruction and damage to the trees.[129] The net effect of the

Court's holding is to determine damages by using the value of the trees that were destroyed or injured on the property.

Similarly, in *Barker v. Publishers' Paper Co.*,[130] the Court allowed the aesthetic loss of the plaintiff's use of the property as a summer school as an element to be considered in assessing the depreciation of the value of the property caused by the defendant's wrongfully cutting down trees on the property and using the site as a sawmill.[131] However, the Court in *Barker* pointed out that the plaintiff could recover the aesthetic value of the land, less the practical value of the property in its damaged condition, or he could recover the value of the use by the defendant for sawmill purposes, but he could not recover both as this would result in the duplication of damages.[132]

In *Zwick v. Simpson*,[133] an action was brought to recover damages for a water drainage problem and the loss of a tree allegedly caused by construction on adjoining property. The Court in *Zwick* recognized the general rule in assessing the measure of damages to real property to be the difference between the fair market value of the property before and after an injury occurs.[134] However, the Court held that a deviation from such a measure would be permitted where the circumstances indicate that repair or restoration costs more accurately reflect the actual loss suffered.[135]

As the authority cited indicates, ordinarily the measure of damages resulting from the destruction of trees is the resulting depreciation in the value of the land on which the trees stood. However, various factors are also considered as affecting the depreciation in the value of the land including the value of the destroyed or injured trees, the cost of replacing the trees themselves or of restoring the premises to its previous condition and sometimes even the resulting loss of aesthetic value to the land.

Under what circumstances will the cost of restoration resulting from the loss of trees be used?

Under certain circumstances, the courts have found it appropriate to use the cost of restoration of the property to its former condition in assessing damages resulting from the destruction or injury to trees. For example, in *Farny v. Bestfield Buildings, Inc.*,[136] the Court found that an appropriate measure of damages was the cost of restoration. In *Farny*, the purchasers of land brought an action for damages against a builder for the destruction of trees on the property occurring in the course of construction on their home. The Trial Court determined that the measure of damages would be the value of the property with the trees less the value of the property without the trees.

On appeal, the Appellate Court in *Farny* did recognize that the measure of damages for trespass of land is the difference between the value of the land before the trespass occurred and the value of the land after the trespass. However, the Court in *Farny* further held that in an appropriate case, the jury may properly consider both the costs of restoration and the before and after valuation of the land itself. The Court held that allowing a jury to consider more than one measure of damages would permit flexibility and achieve just and reasonable results. The Court in *Farny* did qualify its holding by stating that replacement costs may be considered only to the extent that the cost is reasonable and practical.[137]

An application of the Court's ruling in *Farny* can be found in the case of *Fiske v. Maczik*.[138] In *Fiske*, an owner of land brought an action against the defendant's nursery for the wrongful removal of a total of fifty-five palm trees from the owner's land. The Court in *Fiske* also recognized the rule in assessing damages to be computed by the loss of value of the land.[139] However, the Court in *Fiske* further held that the proper measure of recovery for the wrongful removal of the trees on the owner's land should be the reasonable cost of replacing the trees removed since replacement in kind, size and condition of these trees was feasible.[140]

Under what circumstances will the value of the injured or destroyed trees be used?

The courts have also held that an appropriate measure of damages could be the value of the trees themselves. For example, in *Adams v. State of Louisiana*,[141] a husband and wife brought an action against the Highway Department for cutting down their landmark Pecan tree. The Pecan tree in question was shaped like the statue of liberty and grew near the right-of-way of the state highway traversing the front of the plaintiffs' property.

The Court in *Adams* ruled that while the tree in question was found to have been seventy-percent decayed or damaged, it was a live and growing tree. The Court said that the award of Seven Hundred Dollars ($700.00) for the value of the tree was not an abuse of discretion, even though the plaintiffs' experts testified that the tree had a value in excess of Three Thousand Two Hundred Dollars ($3,200.00). From the language of the Court's holding, it is obvious that the Court assessed damages according to the value of the tree alone and did not even consider the resulting diminution in the value of the land.[142]

A case which also presented an exception to the general rule that damages for the destruction or injury to trees are to be measured by the difference in the value of the land immediately before and immediately after the destruction is *Lucas v. Morrison*.[143] In *Lucas*, an action was brought to recover damages for the wrongful destruction of a tree growing on the plaintiff's property which had been used to provide shade for the plaintiff's cows. The Court in *Lucas* held that trees growing upon land are a part of the realty, unless they have a market value when detached from the land, and ordinarily the measure of damages for the wrongful destruction of such trees is the difference in the value of the land immediately before the trees were destroyed and immediately after their destruction. However, the Court found that the tree's value in proportion to the value of the entire farm was of such insignificance as not to affect the market value of the land. The Court in *Lucas* held that under these circumstances an exception should be made to the general rule of measure of damages and that the plaintiff should be entitled to the intrinsic value of his shade tree.[144]

An excellent case which illustrates a method of assessing damages based upon the value of live trees is the case of *United States v. Anthony F. Scarry*.[145] During the summer of 1986, the Defendant, Anthony F. Scarry, cut down approximately 60 Gamble Oak trees from the Prescott National Forest, which he subsequently sold for firewood. As a result, federal criminal charges were brought against Mr. Scarry for theft and injury to United States property under Title 18, United States Code, Section 641 and 1361.[146]

In the prosecution of Mr. Scarry, the government introduced evidence of damage beyond the loss of the timber itself. The government relied upon expert testimony from tree and landscape consultant and appraiser, Eugene Eyerly. Mr. Eyerly consulted with the Forest Service officials and wildlife biologists to determine the benefits to the forest provided by the Gamble Oak trees—which was a factor to be considered in the valuation of the trees. The wildlife biologists informed Mr. Eyerly that the Gamble Oak tree produces mast or acorns which is extremely valuable to turkeys, deer and many other species of animals in the national forest. Finally, Mr. Eyerly physically inspected the damaged area to determine the condition and location of the trees.[147]

At the time of trial, testimony was introduced and accepted by the Court of the value of the live trees in terms of their lost contribution to the forest ecosystem. This value was estimated at $33,812.00. Title 18, United States Code, Section 641 and 1361, provide that if the damage exceeds $100.00 then a felony conviction can be sustained. Mr. Scarry was convicted under both Sections of the Federal Criminal Code.[148]

The *Scarry* case is interesting not only in its illustration of the method used to assess damages but also in the fact that it points out that civil damages are not the only sanctions which are imposed in cases involving an unlawful removal of trees. Criminal sanctions are also available. State criminal statutes for damages and injuries to trees have been included in Appendix II for the reader's edification.

Under what circumstances will the loss of aesthetic value of the trees be used?

The courts have also held that the loss of aesthetic value the trees provided to the landowner can be used in assessing damages for the destruction of shade or ornamental trees. For example, in *Turner v. Southern Excavation, Inc.*,[149] a landowner brought an action against the defendant excavation company for damages as a result of the company's willful, reckless and wanton trespass. The lot was covered with small trees and shrubbery. Trees identified specifically as having been growing on the property before being destroyed by the defendant included Cedar, Plum, Peach and Crepe Myrtle. Of particular relevance is the fact that many of the fruit trees were bearing.

The Court in *Turner* held that neither the cost of replacement nor the diminution in market value was an appropriate measure of damages under the circumstances presented since the former was out of proportion to the market value and the latter would have been too low to properly compensate the landowner. The Court recognized the right of property owners to recover damages which take away from the aesthetic value of their property. A factor which the Court took into consideration in this case in the assessment of damages was the fact that the landowner visited the property weekly to view the trees which had been planted by the landowner's late husband and which had sentimental and aesthetic value.[150] It would seem that the Court placed great significance on the fact that these trees were irreplaceable to the landowner and that their only discernible value was the value as perceived by the landowner herself.

In *Williams v. Hanover Insurance Company of New York*,[151] an action was brought to recover damages to a Live Oak tree caused when an automobile of the defendant's insured collided with a tree some five years before the trial. The Court in *Williams* held that the measure of damages to a large Live Oak tree which aesthetically enhanced the appearance of the plaintiff's well-landscaped yard was the loss of aesthetic value during the period of the tree's recovery.[152] The Court noted that the tree had been injured five years previously when an automobile collided with it and that the defendant's tree surgeon predicted that the tree would recover fully within one or two years. The Court in assessing damages to the Oak tree took into consideration the fact that the aesthetic depreciation in the tree in the latter years of the tree's recovery would not be so great as in the earlier years. With these considerations in mind, the Court awarded damages in the amount of Seven Hundred

Dollars ($700.00) based on the loss of aesthetic value to the plaintiff's property.[153]

Is the tree owner ever provided with a choice as to the measure of damages to be used?

Yes, a case in which the court offered the tree owner with a choice in relation to the method used to measure damages for the wrongful destruction of the owner's trees was *Denoyer v. Lamb*.[154] In *Denoyer*, a property owner brought an action for the cutting and destruction of timber on the landowner's property by a logger who had only been licensed to work on adjoining property. In assessing the measure of damages for the removal of the trees, the trial Court excluded evidence of the costs of clean-up and restoration and restricted the landowner to proof of the timber and stumpage value of the cut and destroyed trees.

On appeal, the upper Court ruled that in an action for compensatory damages for cutting, destroying and damaging trees when the owner intends to use the property for a residence or for recreation or both, the owner is not limited to the diminution in value to the land or to the stumpage value of the timber. The Court further held that a landowner could recover as damages the costs of reasonable restoration of the property to its pre-existing condition or to a condition as close as reasonably feasible, without requiring grossly disproportionate expenditures. The Court in *Denoyer* gave the owner the option as to which measure of damages would be used to determine the owner's loss. The Court's basis for such a holding is that an injured party should be fully compensated for such party's damages, therefore, allowing a landowner to choose an alternative in assessing damages which would best provide for complete compensation.[155]

Will the commercial value of the tree's timber ever be used in measuring damages?

Yes, this issue was addressed by the Court in the *Denoyer* case. The Court ruled that timber cut or to be cut for commercial purposes may be valued in several ways: stumpage is the value of the undistributed timber standing or lying on the land; add to that the cost of filling and hauling to find the value of the logs; add to that again all costs of manufacture to obtain the finished product. The Court recognized that valuation of this type is appropriate to the owner who holds land in order to exploit its timber.[156] Therefore, under certain circumstances the courts will use the commercial value of trees grown for sale as a measure of damages when trees have been wrongfully cut.

Although various measures have been applied by the courts where damages have been sought for the destruction of or injury to trees, it is quite apparent from the courts' opinions that the prevailing view is to assess damage based on the resulting depreciation in the value of the land on which the trees stood. As discussed, there is authority which recognizes alternative methods of measuring damages such as the cost of restoration and replacement of the trees and the loss of aesthetic value to the land. However, the courts which have used those alternative measures all began their opinions by recognizing that the general rule for assessing damages is the resulting depreciation in the value of the land on which the trees stood. The courts have used alternative methods of assessing damages only in appropriate circumstances where the tree owner would not be adequately compensated if the depreciation in the value of the land method was used.

Are there damages which the tree owner is entitled to recover separate and apart from compensatory and punitive damages?

Yes, the *Denoyer* case also addressed the tree owner's right to recover damages separate and apart from compensatory and punitive damages. The Court in *Denoyer* recognized the fact that the State of Ohio had a statute which makes a person liable in treble damages for the injury caused by the reckless cutting, destruction or otherwise injury to shrubs, saplings, and trees growing on the land of another. The Court in *Denoyer* made clear the fact that in order for the tree owner to recover treble damages the owner must show that the destructive acts were done recklessly in accordance with how that term is defined under the state's statute providing for the definition of the term "reckless".

Many states have statutes similar to that of Ohio and many of these statutes have been listed in the attached Appendix II for the reader's edification.

Chapter 10
Conclusion

The law pertaining to the rights, duties and damages of a landowner in relation to trees growing on the landowner's property appears to be straight forward. The landowner is exempt from liability for injuries caused by trees resulting from natural conditions, but the landowner will be responsible for injuries which the landowner could have taken measures to prevent. In essence, the law in this area is really in accord with basic principles of negligence generally found in situations concerning premises liability. With regard to damages for the unauthorized destruction of or injury to a landowner's trees, the law in this area also appears to be in accord with general principles of law concerning compensatory damages. The courts recognize that a landowner has a property interest in trees for which compensation lies when an unauthorized destruction or injury occurs, just the same as when an unauthorized destruction or injury occurs to any other property interest held by an individual.

While the law in relation to trees appears to be clear and straight forward, this fact seems inconsistent in light of the extensive litigation that takes place in this area. Perhaps a reason for the abundant litigation which occurs results from a lack of knowledge which the average individual has in relation to trees. Trees are viewed as natural conditions growing on one's land. Their existence and condition are both taken for granted. A landowner's focus is primarily on the aesthetic aspects which a tree brings to the landowner's property rather than on the possible injuries which such trees may inflict upon others. A landowner's lack of knowledge concerning the landowner's duty in relation to trees growing on the landowner's property results in a failure by the landowner to take preventive measures in order to protect others from injuries which result from such trees. Along the same line of thought, the average individual often engages in the unauthorized destruction of another's trees due to the fact that the individual is unaware of the property interest that a landowner has in such trees. It is difficult for the average person to conceptualize any actual dollar value associated with trees. This is particularly true in cases concerning trees growing on residential property. Imagine, if you will, the surprise which poor Mrs. Shirley Groover of Highlands Park, Illinois received when she paid two men $300.00 cash to chop down 44 trees to create a lake view from her ravine-top home. The $300.00 lake view was to have been a surprise for Mrs. Groover's husband. Unfortunately, the surprise was on Mrs. Groover. Even more unfortunate was the fact that the 44 trees which Mrs. Groover paid to have cut down were not on her property but, rather, 32 of them belonged to the City and the other 12 belonged to her neighbor. Mrs. Groover's $300.00 surprise for her husband has made her a defendant in a $31,000.00 lawsuit brought against her by the City of Highland Park. This is but a single example of the type of cases which flood the courts each year due to the lack of knowledge by the general public of legal issues regarding trees.

However, property owners are not the only ones who have difficulty in interpreting the nature of the rights and values associated with trees. Municipalities and public utilities are also frequent parties to litigation resulting either from their failure to act or through their action without authority. Unfortunately, the courts are even confused with regard to tree-related cases. The courts have placed great emphasis on whether trees are of natural growth in determining the possible liabilities resulting from tree-related injures. In assessing damages for the destruction to trees, the courts have invariably used the resulting depreciation to the land method in determining damages. The courts' rationale for using this method is that basically the principle value of the tree can only be ascertained by making a determination as to what value they impart to the realty on which they stand. Based on this rationale, it appears that courts also take the actual value of trees for granted. This fact, in effect, reinforces many of the uncertainties held by landowners and other individuals concerning actual values which can be placed on trees. Based on the foregoing, it is apparent that there exists a need for educating the public with regard to the rights, liabilities and values to be associated with trees. Knowledge and a greater awareness of the law in this area may provide a solution in decreasing the vast litigation which occurs with regard to trees.

It is, perhaps, appropriate to conclude with the following which was taken from the text of an appellate court's poetic decision arising out of a claim for damages to a tree:

"We thought that we would never see
A suit to compensate a tree;

A suit whose claim in tort is pressed
Upon a mangled tree's behest;

A tree whose battered trunk was pressed
Against a Chevy's crumpled crest;

A tree that faces each new day
With bark and limb in disarray;

A tree that may forever bear
A lasting need for tender care;

Flora lovers though we three,
We must uphold the court's decree

Affirmed."[157]

Table of Cases Cited

1. 166 A.2d 743 (D.C. Mun. App. 1961).
2. *Id.*
3. 144 A.2d 269 (D.C. Mun. App. 1958).
4. *Id.*
5. 55 F.2d 231 (3d Dir. 1931).
6. *Id.*
7. 199 Miss.175, 24 So.2d 356 (1946).
8. *Id.*
9. 75 A.2d 144 (D.C. Mun. App. 1950).
10. *Id.*
11. 42 NY 484 (1870).
12. *Id.*
13. 198 Okla. 896, 181 P.2d 568 (1947).
14. *Id.*
15. 289 S.W.2d 447 (Mo. App. 1956).
16. *Id.*
17. 4 App. Div. 198, 38 N.Y.S. 554 (1896).
18. *Id.*
19. *Id.*
20. 104 Ind. App.118, 9 N.E.2d 114 (1937).
21. *Id.*
22. *Id.*
23. 62 Ohio St.3d 138, 404 N.E.2d 742 1980.
24. *Id.*
25. *Id.*
26. *Id.*
27. 7 Ohio App.3d 110, 454 N.E.2d 564 (1982).
28. *Id.*
29. *Id.*
30. *Id.*
31. 9 Ohio St.3d 194, 459 N.E.2d 873 (1984).
32. *Id.*
33. 374 So.2d. 265 (1979).
34. *Id.*
35. *Id.*
36. *Id.*
37. *Id.*
38. *Id.*
39. 7 Cal. App.39, 93 P.383 (1907).
40. *Id.*

41. 65 Conn. 365, 32 A.939 (1895).
42. *Id.*; *Phillips v. Brittingham*, 25 Del. 173, 77 A.964 (1910), *Blalock v. Atwood*, 154 Ky.394, 157 S.W. 694 (1913).
43. 161 Colo. 337, 421 P.2d 729 (1966).
44. 138 Neb. 656, 294 N.W. 448 (1940).
45. *Id.*
46. 80 Utah 409, 15 P.2d 340 (1932).
47. *Id.*
48. 22 Conn. Supp. 189, 164 A.2d 859 (1960).
49. *Id.*
50. 98 Ind. App.15, 187 N.E. 63 (1933).
51. 304 P.2d 1001 (Okla. 1956).
52. *Id.*
53. 78 *Idaho 822, 306 P.2d 1091 (1957).*
54. *Id.*
55. 78 Cal. 611, 21 P.366 (1889).
56. *Id.*
57. 65 Conn. 365, 32 A.939 (1895).
58. *Id.*
59. 35 Ohio Op. 135, 74 N.E.2d 648 (1947).
60. *Id.*
61. 112 Cal. App.2d 1, 345 P.2d 617 (1952).
62. *Id.*
63. *Id.*
64. 275 Mass. 232, 175 N.E. 490 (1931).
65. *Id.*
66. 116 Wash. 228, 199 P.298 (1921).
67. *Id.*
68. *Id.*
69. 22 Cal. App.3d 116 (1971).
70. 178 Cal. App.3d 1147 (1986).
71. *Id.*
72. *Id.*
73. *Id.*
74. *Id.*
75. *Id.*
76. 324 Mass. 327, 86 N.E.2d 511 (1949).
77. *Id.*
78. 85 Conn. 128, 81 A. 958 (1911).
79. *Id.*
80. 156 Mich. 630, 121 N.W. 490 (1909).
81. Ohio Attorney General Opinion 2210 (1961).

82. 15 Ohio St.3d 402, 473 N.E.2d 1204 (1984).
83. *Id.*
84. *Id.*
85. 92 Ohio App. 14, 109 N.E.2d 481 (1951).
86. *Id.*
87. *Bentley v. Saunemin Township*, 83 Ill.2d 10, 413 N.E.2d 1242 (1980); *Lorig v. Mission*, 629 S.W.2d 699 (1982); *Cooper v. Southern Pines*, 58 N.C. App. 170, 293 S.E.2d 235 (1982).
88. *Shavin v. Tucson*, 17 Ariz. App.16, 495 P2d 841 (1972); *Royce v. Smith*, 680 Ohio St.2d 106, 429 N.E.2d 134 (1981).
89. *Jenkins v. Alexandria*, 324 So.2d 924 (La App.1975); *Nakamara v. Jeffrey*, 6 Wash. App.274, 492 P.2d 244 (1972).
90. 83 Ill.2d 10, 413 N.E.2d 1242 (1980).
91. 130 Ill. App.3d 275, 413 N.E.2d 83 (1985).
92. *Id.*
93. 205 Mo. 126, 103 S.W. 982 (1907).
94. *Id.*
95. 51 Ohio St. 348, 37 N.E. 710 (1894).
96. *Id.*
97. 18 Ohio St.2d 101, 247 N.E.2d 728 (1969).
98. *Id.*
99. 14 Ohio App.3d 421, 471 N.E.2d 825 (1984).
100. *Id.*
101. *Id.*
102. 183 Tenn. 123, 191 S.W.2d 175 (1945).
103. *Id.*
104. 94 So.2d 809 (Fla. 1957).
105. *Id.*
106. 3 Ohio App.3d 153, 444 N.E.2d 77 (1981).
107. *Liability for Injury Involving Trees* by Dr. Walter S. Barrows, Sr., October 1989.
108. *Marion J. Gilbreath v. Veldkamp's Flowers, Inc.*, District Court of Jefferson, State of Colorado, Civil Action No. 83CV0072 (1983).
109. *Id.*
110. *Steven S. Roberts et al. v. Colorado Weed Control et al.*, District Court, Douglas County, Colorado, Civil Action No. 80CV183, Division 9 (1982).
111. *Id.*
112. *Id.*
113. *Id.*
114. *Id.*

115. *Alvin A. Sellon et al. v. Thornton Flying Service*, District Court, Morgan County, State of Colorado, Case No. 83CV115 (1983).
116. *Id.*
117. *Id.*
118. *Id.*
119. 514 N.E.2d 902 (1986).
120. *Id.*
121. *Id.*
122. 306 Minn. 155, 235 N.W.2d 613 (1975).
123. *Id.*
124. *Id.*
125. 21 Ohio App.2d 41, 254 N.E.2d 703 (1970).
126. *Id.*
127. *Id.*
128. 226 Ark. 961, 295 S.W.2d 768 (1956).
129. *Id.*
130. 78 N.H. 571, 103 A.757 (1918).
131. *Id.*
132. *Id.*
133. 37 Colo. App.430, 851 P.2d 216 (1976), 572 P.2d 133 (1977).
134. *Id.*
135. *Id.*
136. 391 A.2d 212 (Del. 1978).
137. *Id.*
138. 329 So.2d 35 (Fla. App. 1976).
139. *Id.*
140. *Id.*
141. 357 So.2d 1239 (La. App.2d Cir. 1978).
142. *Id.*
143. 286 S.W.2d 190 (Tex. Civ. App. 1956).
144. *Id.*
145. *United States v. Anthony F. Scarry*, No. 88-1251, D.C. No. CR-87-0326-PGR (9th Cir. 1989).
146. *Id.*
147. *Id.*
148. *Id.*
149. 322 So.2d 326 (La. App.2d Cir. 1975).
150. *Id.*
151. 351 So.2d 858 (La. App.2d Cir. 1977).
152. *Id.*
153. *Id.*
154. 22 Ohio App.3d 136, 490 N.E.2d 615 (1984).

155. *Id*.
156. *Id*.
157. 122 Mich. App. 418, 333 N.W.2d 67 (1983).

Appendix I
Definition of Terms

Act of God   An act occasioned exclusively by violence of nature without the interference of any human agency

Actual damages   The amount of damages awarded to a complainant in compensation for his actual and real loss or injury

Boundary line tree   A tree owned in common by two adjoining landowners either through course of conduct or proximity to property lines

Common law   Principles and rules of action relating to the government of persons and property which derive their authority from judgments and decrees of the court

Compensatory damages   Damages that will compensate the injured party for the loss caused by the wrong or injury

Contributory negligence   The conduct by an individual which is below the standard to which he is legally required to conform for his own protection and which is a contributing cause resulting in his own harm

Covenant   An agreement or promise of two or more parties by deed in writing by which either of the parties agrees that something is either done, will be done or will not be done

Defendant   The party against whom relief or recovery is sought in an action or lawsuit

Easement   An interest and right of use one person has over the property of another

Enjoined   To require a person, by an act of court, to abstain or desist from some act

Injunction   A judicial order requiring a person to whom it is directed to do or refrain from doing a particular thing

Joint and several liability   A person who has been harmed can recover damages from both wrongdoers or from either one of the wrongdoers

Licensee   A person who is privileged to enter or remain upon land for a specific purpose by virtue of the possessor's consent, whether given by invitation or permission

Natural condition   A condition not in any way the result of human activity

Negligence   The failure to use such care as a reasonably prudent person would use under similar circumstances

Negligence per se   Conduct which may be declared as negligence without any argument or proof as to the particular surrounding circumstances, either because it is a violation of a statute or valid municipal ordinance

Nuisance   An activity which arises from unreasonable, unwarranted, or unlawful use by a person of his own property which causes obstruction or injury to the property rights of another

Ordinance   The equivalent of a municipal statute, passed by the city council or equivalent body, governing matters not already covered by federal or state law

Plaintiff   A person who brings a lawsuit or action for injuries to his rights

Prudence   Carefulness, precaution, attentiveness, and good judgment, as applied to action or conduct

Punitive damages   Damages other than compensatory damages awarded to punish acts for outrageous conduct

Reasonable care   That degree of care which a person of ordinary prudence would exercise in the same or similar circumstances

Reasonable foreseeability   The reasonable anticipation that harm or injury is a likely result of acts or omissions

Reasonable man standard   The standard which one must observe to avoid liability for neligence; what the reasonable man would do under all the circumstances encompassing the foreseeability of harm that could result to another by a certain act

Statute   An act of the legislature declaring, commanding, or prohibiting something

Tenants in common   Two or more individuals who hold the same land together by several and distinct title but by unity of possession

Treble damages   Damages given by statute in certain cases consisting of the single damages found by the jury and tripled in amount.

Trespass   The unlawful interference with the property or rights of another

Wanton conduct   The reckless disregard for the rights and safety of others

Appendix II

Various State Statutes Which Provide Damages Recoverable for Injuries to Trees

Actual loss

Georgia	Ga. Code Ann. 5 1-12-50

Double damages

Mississippi	Miss. Code Ann 95-5-10
Pennsylvania	18 Pa. Con. Stat. 1107
Rhode Island	R.I. Gen. Laws 34-20-1 (sometimes triple)
Wisconsin	Wis. Stat. Ann. 26.09

Triple Damages

Alaska	Alaska Stat. Ann. 09.45.730
Arkansas	Ark. Code Ann. 18-60-102
California	Cal. Civ. Code 3346
Connecticut	Conn. Gen. Stat. Ann. 52-560
Delaware	Del. Code Ann. 25-1401
Idaho	Idaho Code Ann. 6-202
Illinois	Ill. Stat. Ann. Ch. 96 ½ Section 9402
Iowa	Ia. Code Ann. 658.4
Louisiana	La. Civ. Code 3:4278.1
Maine	14 Me. Rev. Stat. Ann. 7552
Maryland	Md. Code Ann. N.R. 5-409
Minnesota	Minn. Stat. Ann. 561.04
Missouri	Mo. Stat. Ann. 537.340
Montana	Mont. Code Ann. 70-16-108
Nebraska	Rev. Stat. Neb. 25-2130

Triple Damages (cont.)

Nevada	Nev. Rev. Stat. 40.160
New York	Con. Laws N.Y. Ann. R.P.A.P.L. 861
North Dakota	N.D. Cent. Code Ann. 32-03-30
Ohio	Ohio Rev. Code Ann. 901.51
Oklahoma	23 Okla. Stat. Ann. 572
Oregon	Ore. Rev. Stat. 105.810
South Dakota	S.D. Comp. Laws Ann. 21-3-10
Utah	Utah Code Ann. 78-38-3
Vermont	13 Vt. Stat. Ann. 3606
Washington	Rev. Code Wash. Ann. 64.12.030
West Virginia	W. Va. Code Ann. 61-3-48a

Five times the amount of damages

New Hampshire	N.H. Rev. Stat. Ann. 539.1

Punitive damages

Kentucky	Ken. Rev. Stat. 364.130

Fines or jail sentences for damaging a tree

Alabama	Ala. Code Ann. 35-14-1
California	Ca. Pen. Code Section 384a
Delaware	Del. Code Ann. 7-3301
District of Columbia	D.C. Code Ann. 22-3108
Idaho	Idaho Code Ann. 18-7021
Massachusetts	Mass. Gen. Laws Ann. Ch. 266 Sections 113,114
Michigan	Mich. Comp. Laws Ann. 750.382
New Jersey	N.J. Stat. Ann. 2C.18-5
New Mexico	N.M. Stat. Ann. 68-2-22,23
North Carolina	N.C. Gen. Stat. 14-128

Fines or jail sentences for damaging a tree (cont.)

Ohio	Ohio Rev. Code Ann. 901.99
Oklahoma	21 Okla. Stat. Ann. 1768
Oregon	Ore. Rev. Stat. 527.260
Rhode Island	R.I. Gen. Laws 11-44-2
South Carolina	Code of Laws S.C. 16-11-520
Virginia	Code of Va. 18.2-140
Wisconsin	Wis. Stat. Ann. Sections 814.04,26.05

States which have no statutes regarding injuries to trees;

Arizona

Colorado

Florida

Indiana

Kansas

Tennessee

Texas

Wyoming

Appendix III
State Statutes Which Outline Private Nuisance

Alabama	Ala. Code Ann. 6-5-120 (slightly different language)
California	Cal. Civ. Code Section 3479
Georgia	Ga. Code Ann. 41-1-1 (slightly difference language)
Idaho	Idaho Code Ann. 52-111
Indiana	Ann. Ind. Code 34-1-52-1
Iowa	Ia. Code Ann. 657.1
Minnesota	Minn. Stat. Ann. 561.01
Montana	Mont. Code Ann. 27-30-101
New Jersey	N.J. Stat. Ann. 2C:33-12 (limiting public nuisance)
New Mexico	N.M. Stat. Ann. 30-8-1 (limiting public nuisance)
Nevada	Nev. Rev. Stat. 40.140
North Dakota	N.D. Cent. Code Ann. 42-01-01
Oklahoma	50 Okla. Stat. Ann. 1
South Dakota	S.D. Comp. Laws Ann. 21-10-1
Utah	Utah Code Ann. 78-38-1
Washington	Rev. Code Wash. Ann. 7.48.010

Appendix IV
Checklists for Practicing Arborists

I. Facts and circumstances which tend to establish that the property owner failed to exercise due care in maintenance of trees:

   A. Urban/Rural location of tree
   B. Tree's growth as natural
   C. Dangerous characteristics of tree
   D. Visible and apparent dangerous condition of tree
   E. Property owner's knowledge of dangerous condition of tree
   F. Dead and rotten condition of tree disclosed by examination and inspection

II. Damages recoverable for injuries caused by trees:

   A. Costs of removing debris of fallen tree
   B. Market value of property destroyed by fallen tree
   C. Costs of repairs to property injured by fallen tree
   D. Value of trees and other vegetation injured or destroyed by fallen tree
   E. Value of animals killed
   F. Wrongful death actions for individuals killed
   G. Medical expenses, pain and suffering, and lost wages for individuals injured.

III. Damages recoverable for injuries to trees:

   A. Resulting depreciation in the value of the land
   B. Cost of restoration
   C. Value of tree
   D. Aesthetic value of tree
   E. Commercial value of tree's timber
   F. Reduction in rental value of commercial property
   G. Punitive damages
   H. Damages proscribed by statute

IV. Where to locate state statutes and municipal ordinances:

   A. State statutes—County law libraries, law school libraries, and city public libraries.
   B. City municipal ordinances—City halls, county courthouses, county law libraries, and city public libraries.

MTR/881

About the Authors

Victor D. Merullo is a senior partner in the law firm of Merullo, Reister & Swinford Co., L.P.A. located in Columbus, Ohio. He has been in the public and private practice of law for nineteen years following his graduation from Capital University Law School with a Juris Doctorate Degree. In the public practice of law, he worked for the Ohio Attorney General, assigned primarily to the Ohio Department of Agriculture. In the private practice of law, he has handled cases in various aspects of the law including numerous matters relating to tree related problems. He has been a featured speaker on legal issues relating to the law of trees across the United States. He studied horticulture at Ohio State University while working in his family's businesses, devoted primarily to arboriculture, interior and exterior landscaping. He is considered a leading expert in the law of trees and authored the first publication devoted exclusively to the law of trees.

Michael J. Valentine is an associate in Victor D. Merullo's law firm. He received a Juris Doctorate Degree from Capital University Law School in Columbus, Ohio. He has been involved in numerous cases dealing with tree related problems, including litigation relating to damages to trees. He has engaged in extensive research concerning various aspects of the law as it pertains to trees throughout the United States.